Synthetic
Fuel Technology
Development in
the United States

Synthetic Fuel Technology Development in the United States

A Retrospective Assessment

MICHAEL CROW
BARRY BOZEMAN
WALTER MEYER
RALPH SHANGRAW, JR.

PRAEGER

New York
Westport, Connecticut
London

Library of Congress Cataloging-in-Publication Data

Synthetic fuel technology development in the United
   States.
   Bibliography: p.
   Includes index.
   1. Synthetic fuels—United States.   I. Crow,
Michael M.
TP360.S9365   1988   333.79'15'0973   88–12596
ISBN 0–275–93083–1 (alk. paper)

Library of Congress Catalog Card Number: 88–12596
ISBN: 0–275–93083–1

First published in 1988

Praeger Publishers, One Madison Avenue, New York, NY 10010
A division of Greenwood Press, Inc.

Printed in the United States of America

The paper used in this book complies with the
Permanent Paper Standard issued by the National
Information Standards Organization (Z39.48–1984).

10 9 8 7 6 5 4 3 2 1

CONTENTS

LIST OF TABLES AND FIGURES

TABLES

FIGURES

PREFACE

There is some agreement that synthetic liquid fuels will be required for the twenty-first century energy economy. Direct coal liquefaction (DCL) is one of the major developmental alternatives for meeting anticipated synfuel demands. The urgency of the need to examine the development climate for direct coal liquefaction depends upon one's view of just when in the next century the need for synthetic fuels will become critical and just what kind of role DCL should play in meeting energy needs.

This effort began with no unalterable assumptions about these questions but is motivated by a recognition of the importance of the issues of need and timing. The approach taken here assumes that one of the most instructive means of inquirying about present and future technology development needs and strategies is to examine past ones. Specifically, a retrospective technology assessment is performed to assess the key determinants of the previous stages of DCL development.

WHAT IS RETROSPECTIVE TECHNOLOGY ASSESSMENT?

Technology assessment (TA) has been defined as "a class of policy studies which systematically examine the effects on society that may occur when a technology is introduced, extended or modified."[1] As a self-conscious and systematic enterprise, technology assessment is no more than twenty years old. By this time, hundreds of large-scale technology assessments have been performed. While these studies have focused on a wide variety of topics, most have been "anticipatory" technology assessments in the sense that they have sought to predict the impacts of technological development.

Retrospective technology assessment (RTA) is a methodological invention even more recent in origin than traditional TA. The most obvious way in which RTA differs from traditional TA is in its historical focus. The fact that RTA examines events in history, rather than current impacts and possible future impacts, provides some distinct advantages and disadvantages. The success of an RTA depends greatly on the ability to make decisions about novel methodological issues.

In one of the few existing works detailing the RTA methodology, Mary Hamilton suggests a seven step approach to RTA. Those seven steps include:

1. The technology and the context of the technology development are defined.
2. Based on those definitions, data sources are identified.
3. A questionnaire to "interview" the data sources is formulated and applied.
4. Based on the results of applying the questionnaire, a "standard development case" is applied.
5. Notable exceptions to aspects of the standard development case are identified, described, and documented, and the conditions under which they occurred are described.
6. If there are sufficient notable exceptions, one or more "alternative development cases" are developed.
7. A "standard baseline [nondevelopment] case" is formulated by means of the same questionnaire approach.[2]

HOW IS RETROSPECTIVE TECHNOLOGY ASSESSMENT APPLIED HERE?

The methodological approach taken here is a variant of that described above. First, three different analytical models are assumed as explanations of DCL development. A *technology model* assumes that the best understanding of DCL development comes from a knowledge of the scientific and technical evolution of DCL. A *policy model* assumes that government policy and actors must be understood. Finally, an *economics model* assumes that economic factors have been of paramount importance in determining the developmental course for DCL.

For each of the three models Hamilton's "interviewing the data" approach is employed. A series of questions is formulated and the answers to these questions drive the analysis. The questions are answered by a variety of means including analysis of historical documents, examination of budget and economic data, analysis of patent trends, and, perhaps most important, interviews with DCL experts from industry and government.

As a "baseline case," H-Coal is used as a point of comparison. H-Coal, an approach that is well known and has a history both familiar and checkered, is examined in some detail. The purpose is to have a "microscopic" view of one technology, which may then be employed as a source of hypotheses for other technologies of current interest.

FINDINGS

The findings developed in each of the "model" chapters are synthesized and distilled in Chapter 9. Chief findings include the following:

1. There has been a damaging "hiatus effect" in the development of DCL. The on-again, off-again policies (both public and business policies) for DCL development have drastically undercut the ability to generate knowledge, maintain investments in human capital and equipment, and make technological progress.

2. DCL is not economically competitive, never has been, and shows limited prospects of becoming economically competitive in the near-term (in the absence of any revolutionary breakthroughs in technology or revolutionary changes in the international energy economy). Two perspectives lead to two different conclusions about the lack of economic competitiveness:

   a. If one assumes that DCL will not become a significant energy source in the United States until it is economically competitive with the price of foreign oil (a plausible but not unimpeachable assumption), then the possibilities of payoff from non-revolutionary research are minimal. This seems to suggest a focus on basic research that focuses on elemental coal chemistry.

   2. If one assumes that for the sake of energy security, DCL should be an important energy source for the United States (even if it is not economically competitive), then it is important to provide sustained support to a few technologically (if not economically) viable DCL approaches.

3. The notion of fostering an unsheltered DCL industry has some merits but, from a practical standpoint, has not been a productive strategy. If DCL is important for the present and future energy security of the United States, it should be treated as other public goods—that is, it should not be evaluated exclusively by market criteria. Industry will not develop a technology that is a "loser" in the marketplace and it will not develop a technology just because it has high value as a public good. Previous technology development efforts (in aerospace and in the early computer industries, for example) have achieved important benefits by government procurement policy and by government-guaranteed demand. This same approach could be used to develop DCL if there is an interest in exploiting DCL's potential as an answer to energy security questions.

This effort is, of course, the result of numerous supporters. Scores of engineers, politicians, economists, and others gave both of their time and knowledge to the project. Numerous graduate research assistants at Syracuse University gave their time and talents to collect and analyze some of the information included in the text. Finally, through the support of Dr. Lyle Sendlein at the University of Kentucky and the Consortium for Fossil Fuel Liquefaction Science (a U.S. Department of Energy-funded university research effort), this project was nurtured and developed.

Synthetic Fuel Technology Development in the United States

1 —————— THE CONTEXT OF DIRECT COAL LIQUEFACTION DEVELOPMENT IN THE SYNTHETIC FUELS TECHNOLOGY ARENA

Since the early twentieth century, the government of the United States has implemented four major attempts to assist in the development of a synthetic fuels industry. Central to each of these efforts as well as to the general goal of producing synthetic fuels has been the development of liquid fuels to substitute for the Earth's finite petroleum resources. This goal has largely been the result of the realization that naturally-occurring liquid fuels are scarce, subject to drastic price fluctuations, and of significant value as a feedstock for chemicals and plastics. Because of these factors and because of the realities of the technology development process—long lead times, high-risk capital investment, and technical uncertainty—there is substantial concern regarding the ability of U.S. science and technology enterprises to successfully develop technological solutions to the problem of producing synthetic liquid fuels. Despite the long-standing efforts of government and industry, despite the fact that alternatives to natural fuels must, ultimately, be developed as acceptable substitutes, today's synthetic fuels industry is moribund.

Most observers agree that synthetic fuels remain, even after considerable technological development, economically noncompetitive.[1] Conventional wisdom abounds and offers ready, if incomplete, explanations of the "premature burial" of synthetic fuels. Is the controlling variable the world price of oil, as many have concluded, or are there fundamental problems in the technology development process associated with this type of technology development activity?

In sum, there is some agreement that synthetic liquid fuels will be required for the energy economy within the next fifty to one hundred

1

years. There is also a consensus that coal will play a critical role in meeting this demand. Yet the goal of replacing natural liquid fuels with synthetic liquids has been elusive and the technology options designed to meet this goal have been less than successful.

Our goal is to shed some light on this apparent gap between synfuel expectations and performance, suggesting possible lessons about public policies and the economic and technical dimensions of large-scale technology development efforts. A focus on direct coal liquefaction (DCL) is easily justified. In the first place, the history of DCL in the United States is emblematic of the frustrations experienced by policymakers, technologists, and businessmen seeking to act in concert. The economic, political, and technical problems associated with the Coalcon project in the 1970s,[2] and the H-Coal Project of the 1970s and 1980s,[3] need only be mentioned for the realities of the difficulties associated with coal liquefaction to be a remembrance for everyone associated with the technology. But in addition to its value as a "case study" of large-scale technology development policy, DCL has an inherent importance. More than $1 billion in U.S. government funding has been provided to support DCL, and a similarly large amount has been invested by U.S. industry. This public/private effort has resulted in workable technologies, currently available (though not on a commercial scale). So, one significant reason to re-examine DCL is to suggest ways in which the sizable investment might yet be redeemed in some manner. What are the next steps? If one begins with the assumption (as we do) that it makes no sense to utterly abandon DCL, despite its current noncompetitive status, then it is important to understand where the development process has led, why it has led to its current status, and where it might lead.

The vehicle we use for understanding DCL development, in all its technological, economic, and political complexities, is retrospective technology assessment (RTA).[4] This set of techniques is discussed in the next chapter and its specific application to this study of DCL is discussed in Chapter 3. For present purposes, it is enough to say that RTA does not closely resemble engineering feasibility studies, which often we have included under the rubric "technology assessment," but, instead, seeks to understand technology processes as they are embedded in a socioeconomic context. RTA is, essentially, historical and qualitative in its orientation.

A SNAPSHOT OF DIRECT COAL LIQUEFACTION

As mentioned, this analysis is focused on the subset of synthetic liquid fuel technologies that are based on the direct liquefaction of coal. Known as direct coal liquefaction (DCL), these processes rely on thermal energy and solvents to produce high yields of liquid products from coal. Because of its conceptual simplicity, the scale of the coal resource base in the United States, and the experience gained in the direct liquefaction of coal in Germany earlier in this century, options for the production of synthetic liquids have long been heralded as a technology with significant potential.

When the United States found itself in the midst of a serious liquid fuel price increase in the mid-1970s, it was quick to turn to the first-generation DCL processes as an option to imported oil. The assumption was that the technologies that had permitted the Germans to operate their war machine on DCL-derived synthetic liquids in the 1940s could be quickly put into place as a means of reducing U.S. reliance on natural petroleum resources, which were largely available only from unstable sources. In addition to the German experience, the U.S. government had implemented a small demonstration program in the 1950s and several U.S. oil companies developed small-scale R&D efforts.[5] Within the context of a first-generation technology base and in the midst of the nation's first significant energy crisis, the decision was made to develop several second-generation DCL options, which at the time were thought by many to be within 5–10 years of commercialization. The situation leading up to that decision—technically, institutionally, and politically—as well as the actions taken after the decision was made are the critical variables in understanding why DCL research in the United States today has been reduced to sub-critical funding levels and why there is no continuing program.

THE NEED FOR A COMPREHENSIVE TECHNOLOGY ASSESSMENT OF DCL

It can certainly be said that there is no shortage of "technology assessments" related to DCL. In fact a complete review of the literature since the 1940s indicates a number of assessments of the engineering potential for DCL. Most of these assessments are limited to process analysis.

The knowledge base associated with the assessment of DCL is predominantly engineering in character, and this knowledge base is insufficient for the task of carrying out a comprehensive technology assessment. There is a need for a more comprehensive assessment of DCL as a means of answering the questions regarding the best course of action for future development.

The goals of the retrospective technology assessment undertaken herein are:

1. To develop a chronology of the development of DCL in the United States in the twentieth century. This chronology is intended to provide the background

necessary for explaining the sporadic development of DCL and the difficulties in demonstrating a viable commercial alternative.

2. To identify and define the "technology development environments"[6] which appear to have contributed to the success or failure of various ventures in DCL history.

3. To analyze the development potential, based on the technology development environment, of three selected current DCL options (some of which are only in the early stages of development at this time).

4. To determine the extent to which the development process for DCL has been predominantly technology driven, policy driven, or economically driven, and to consider the ways in which these factors have interacted.

The question of whether current DCL approaches (e.g., co-processing, biological liquefaction) are viable is a function of the current status of DCL as well as the environment in which the technology has evolved. In addition, the future development of any viable technologies is dependent on an improved understanding of the impact and interaction of critical technology development variables.

SYNOPSIS OF DIRECT COAL LIQUEFACTION TECHNOLOGY DEVELOPMENT

Since the late nineteenth century, the basic chemistry has been known for the direct liquefaction of coal. Since the 1930s, the simple chemistry for the development of processes for the direct conversion of coal to liquid fuels and chemicals has been detailed and proven. Following this basic effort at developing the conceptualization of DCL, early process configurations were put together for production of liquid fuels in Germany in the 1920s. These first-generation processes, as well as the basic science efforts in Germany, represent much of the science and technology base of DCL. Much of the simple chemistry as well as the fundamental engineering design for first-generation DCL was proven and tested in production scale facilities before 1945.

Given the science base and technology experience gained by the Germans prior to 1945, it is natural that any effort to further develop the technology would start where they left off. This is of course what began in the United States starting in 1943/44. Following WWII, the U.S. government and several key energy companies acquired much of the knowledge base developed in Germany. This knowledge became useful as a result of post-war oil shortages as well as a desire to further develop DCL technology in the United States. This effort culminated with the development of a DCL demonstration facility at Louisiana, Missouri (1949–1953) and the operation of several smaller facilities by the Carbide and Carbon Chemicals Company between 1952 and 1957. These facilities were essentially an Americanized version of the proven, if still inefficient, German technologies that had been in operation ten years earlier. This effort, between 1949 and 1957, was the first of several attempts to transfer the German technology base to the United States. These attempts are best characterized into the four periods summarized below.

Early U.S. Experimentation (1943–1957)

As World War II entered its fourth year, the knowledge that Germany had developed a technology capable of producing liquid fuels directly from coal began to catch the eye of politicians and policymakers in the United States. U.S. scientists and engineers knew that DCL was feasible; in fact, the research of the U.S. Bureau of Mines indicates some tinkering with the basic concept as early as 1924. In addition, some research had been going on in industry and at universities, particularly the Carnegie Institute of Technology in Pittsburgh, since the Bergius findings of the 1920s and 1930s. These efforts were, however, small in scale and were not directed toward the development of a functioning, cost-effective technology.[7]

The knowledge of the German capability combined with the realization that petroleum resources were vulnerable to supply interruptions and price fluctuations resulted in the development of a plan in the U.S. Department of the Interior to develop and demonstrate the German DCL technology on U.S. coals and with U.S. materials. After several years of debate, a program was established to build small demonstration plants using the basic German designs. Little additional research into the fundamental chemistry was planned and little new development activity was anticipated. The goal of this early effort was to transfer the technology and knowledge base developed in Germany to the United States and to demonstrate this early first generation technology on U.S. coals. All demonstration plants constructed during this period proved to be functional but were very inefficient, both economically (in the sense of the price of the fuel products) and also in the sense of engineering efficiency. Finally, with the apparent need for DCL reduced in the 1950s and the perception that low-price oil was a given (particularly with the large acquisitions of Middle Eastern oil by the major U.S. oil companies), the U.S. effort to demonstrate and develop first-generation DCL technology was ended in 1955. Subsequent demonstration efforts by industry seem to have ended for the most part with the shutdown of the Carbide plant in 1957.

In this initial period of technology development in the United States, first-generation processes were demonstrated using U.S. coals. In other words, U.S. scientists and engineers were successful in their efforts to duplicate the earliest technological configuration for the direct conversion of coal to liquid fuels. There was no real attempt to upgrade the process from the German design and there was little attempt to "Americanize" the process configuration for the different chemistry found in U.S. coals. Perhaps most important was the fact that during this period there was very little basic research conducted or transferred to the technology that could overcome the fundamental efficiency problems present in the German technology. The German technology utilized during WWII was based on simple organic chemistry and this chemistry greatly limited the scientific base on which these processes were designed. It was as a result of this limitation that the German technologies utilized to fuel the Luftwaffe were in fact so inefficient that their viability, outside an economy where natural petroleum was unavailable, was very limited.

In addition to the general lack of basic chemistry underpinning the development of these technologies is the fact that there are significant differences between the chemistry of various coals, certainly North American versus European coals. The result of these differences is that the first-generation plants developed by the Germans were essentially designed to process the feedstock characteristics of European coals. Given the fact that these DCL plants are actually chemical processing plants and given the chemical differences between the feedstock coals, it is little wonder that U.S. attempts to experiment with German technology were less than a complete success.

What this history implies is that the general findings of Bergius were quickly developed into a process configuration without substantial knowledge of the chemistry involved. The result was the development of a process technology that under any normal set of economic conditions would have involved substantially more basic research and a great deal more developmental research. Yes, first-generation DCL processes could produce oil from coal; we can also desalinate salt water into fresh—but neither process technology incorporates sufficient basic knowledge to provide alternatives that might provide realistic process economics.

Not being knowledgeable about the process technology or the basic science on which the process was based, U.S. scientists and engineers proceeded with the demonstration of a technology that was destined never to be efficient. It was a technology that could be operationalized but not at any reasonable cost. The early period of experimentation in the United States proved little other than to demonstrate once again that first-generation DCL processes could indeed work. The result was that there was only limited development in the knowledge or technology base beyond that already provided by the Germans.

The Office of Coal Research: The Institutionalization of Coal Research (1961–1973)

After a five-year hiatus in development efforts by the U.S. government, a second national effort to develop coal into a more useful fuel resource was undertaken. On July 7, 1961, President Kennedy established the Office of Coal Research (OCR) at a modest level. The OCR was established to coordinate the government's efforts in developing coal and as a part of this effort, DCL was considered to be an important end-use for coal. In addition, this effort was established with the thought that the declining coal industry of 1960 could be revitalized, hopefully helping some of the United States' more economically depressed areas (Appalachia, in particular). In fact, social goals as opposed to technical goals were the driving force behind the second technology development push.

Within this office there was a major effort launched to develop new DCL processes as part of a general synthetic fuels development effort. These processes, largely rooted on the Bergius-based first-generation efforts, were intended to reduce the engineering economics of the conversion process and to subsequently reduce the cost of the liquid fuel products. Key to reducing cost and improving process efficiency was the development of processes that could convert the coal at lower temperature and pressure than the first-generation processes. The result of the lowering of process temperatures and pressures would be to lower the overall materials requirements for DCL processes and subsequently to lower the cost.

Although funding was modest, the government set out on the course of developing a number of new options for DCL. Because of the fact that there were some developments within the energy industry related to the development of second generation processes, the government entered into R&D contracts with a number of companies. Between 1961 and 1973, funding levels were so low for this activity that only a limited effort could be mounted. These efforts were designed to extrapolate from the existing technology base and to move empirically toward a second-generation technology. Basic research was carried out at a slightly higher level but not at the level necessary to overcome the fundamental problems present in the first-generation technology.

A principal reason for this continued attempt to develop a technology empirically rather than scientifically is linked to the social goals of the pre-1973 OCR program. The program was designed to provide a means for the rapid recovery of the coal industry and its participants. A fully functional technological option for the direct liquefaction of coal, while certainly an important goal, was secondary to the goal of providing rapid assistance to an ailing industry. The key point here is that the development of DCL technology still required substantial basic knowledge in 1961, just as it did in 1948, and because of the multiple goals associated with the establishment of OCR, basic research was not a politically viable part of the program plan.

Beyond the problem of multiple social goals, which included little room for basic research, was a very fundamental struggle between those associated with the coal industry who wanted to see the cost of production and processing reduced and those who felt that the problems associated with the development of new technologies such as DCL merited significant research attention. The successful development of DCL technologies involved the development of substantial basic knowledge on the chemistry and structure of coal—knowledge that was difficult to obtain due to the low level of contemporary coal science and knowledge that might lead to the development of new, perhaps exotic, technologies. The leadership of the coal industry, at that time, while perhaps sympathetic to the need for basic coal research, were captains of an industry that often experienced a boom-and-bust type of existence and nearly always operated at the margin. The result was an industry that invested little of its own resources into research and spoke out loudly for a government research program that would lower the cost of production. It was this conflict that manifested itself quite strongly in the OCR period and thus limited the development of a basic research program on coal.

Just prior to the oil embargo in the fall of 1973, and as a result of the realization that the need for significant quantities of synthetic liquids might occur in the near term, efforts to develop DCL as a synthetic fuel option were dramatically increased. This period of development for DCL is noted for the initiation of some basic coal science research to support the development process and for the expansion of the search for second-generation processes. Among the key DCL alternatives initiated during this period were: (1) H-Coal (the sample case study used in this retrospective technology assessment); (2) solvent-refined coal; (3) Exxon's donor-solvent process; (4) CFS two-stage liquefaction; (5) zinc halide coal liquefaction; and (6) the Dow Chemical Co. coal liquefaction process. While this list is not complete it does represent the processes that played a key role in the efforts to develop a second-generation DCL technology. It is worth noting that each of the processes mentioned above was a process initially developed at the conceptual level by industry and later, with government funding, jointly developed by industry and the government.

To call this period a systematic attempt to improve on the existing knowledge base and to develop the next-generation technology from this improved knowledge base would be inaccurate. To call this period an organized effort to improve on the existing technology base and to work the bugs out, so to speak, would be a better description of the types of activities undertaken by OCR and its industrial contractors. For reasons that are difficult to identify, the basic knowledge regarding the science of DCL remained an area of secondary interest. The result of this fact was that the development of the second-generation technologies required by the energy economy occurred largely through Edisonian development techniques.

At the close of this period, with the United States on the verge of being made aware of the uncertainties associated with global petroleum supply and demand, there were a number of second-generation processes that had been proven at the bench-scale level. There were no DCL options that had even been tested at the pilot plant level and only one or two could claim to have been evaluated at the process demonstration scale. In a developmental sense, little progress had been made in the twenty years since the Louisiana, Missouri, plant and the science base necessary for the successful implementation of new revolutionary processes had yet to be initiated on a scale sufficient to support the development of DCL technology options. The result of these facts was that the development of DCL as an option for producing synthetic liquid fuels was on a track of evolutionary development from an early process configuration that was not viable in a market economy.

THE OIL SHOCK ERA (1974–1982)

After the oil shock of the autumn of 1973, the government in concert with a number of industrial partners embarked on the course of attempting to develop a number of synthetic fuel options as rapidly as possible. Because of the crisis nature of the period, the projects selected for development were those that in theory had the best chance of providing replacement fuels for the economy in the "short term." DCL—with its immediate end-product being liquid fuels, and with its "successful" first-generation development—was seen by many observers as one of the most important options available.

Because of the crisis environment there was again little opportunity to conduct fundamental research. The result was that only those processes that had been under development in the previous era appeared to be viable as a course of action.

Selected for development on a crisis timetable were the H-Coal (see case study) and SRC options. These second-generation options were immediately scaled up for rapid demonstration and planned commercialization. Because of the lack of science supporting these efforts and because of time frame involved, the projects took on the character of crash programs. Massive increases in funding were requested and received and substantial congressional support was given. In short, DCL technologies went from a sub-critical development environment, characterized by a lack of science or empirical research, to a super critical crash program requiring rapid development and deployment of commercial-scale DCL facilities. This transition, which occurred between October 1973 and the spring of 1974, served to create a technology-development environment that among other things was highly politicized, based on a short time horizon and very high risk. It is important to remember that the DCL processes planned for commercialization within eight to ten years of project initiation were only in the earliest stages of development in 1974, when these plans were developed.

The result was that during this period the development of DCL techniques for synthetic fuel production, as well as most other synthetic fuel processes, was plagued with cost overruns, contract problems, and technological failures. The scale of the second-generation DCL processes proved to be so large and the process conditions so severe that, as was the case with the experimentation period, the technology was essentially not efficient. Yes, the operation of the H-Coal pilot plant and the various other DCL process demonstration units (PDUs) was at least partially successful from a technical perspective. Researchers were able to demonstrate the viability of the processes and to identify the barriers for development. These successes were, however, overshadowed by economic failure and loss of policy support for DCL, which began to occur in 1980.

The reasons for the problems identified above are varied. It is our assessment that these difficulties were the result of: (1) premature development of the various DCL options; (2) insufficient scientific base for successful development; (3) unrealistic and deleterious planning and implementation timetables; and (4) inadequate industrial and governmental coordination. These factors working together with the fact that these technology options are the direct descendents of a technology that by design is not intended to be efficient have allowed the development of DCL to enter its second major hiatus period.

In sum, DCL technology is not much further advanced today than it was in the early 1950s.

Technology on Hold (1982–Present)

With the realization that DCL processes were not going to be the simple answer to the complicated issue of oil replacement and with the realization that the development of alternative sources of oil was perhaps not as time critical as once thought, the drive for DCL diminished rapidly.

Shortly after the development of the Synthetic Fuels Corporation by the Carter administration, policy support for DCL projects and other synthetic fuel options diminished quickly. This was particularly true with the advent of the Reagan administration in 1981 and the "supply-side" assumptions regarding government involvement in development activities. It was the assumption of the Reagan administration that the market was the best mechanism for the development of new technologies and that the role of the government in such activities was to provide a basic research and infratechnology base to help developers.[8] With this logic and with the experiences of the previous periods, it was not difficult to develop a coalition to support the elimination of government support for synthetic fuel development and for the ultimate demise of the Synthetic Fuels Corporation.

The status of DCL technology development in the United States in the late 1980s is that it is essentially returned to the levels of R&D activity common in the early 1960s. The only difference is that now instead of thinking about a range of second-generation options, the program's focus has been reduced to a very limited number of DCL options. What this means is that given all the problems associated with the development of this technology in the past, its future development will in all likelihood be even more difficult. There is no main effort to continue the production of basic knowledge underway or planned, and there is no effort to continue the development of the pilot plants and PDUs that were operated in the previous period.

DCL as a viable option for the production of synthetic liquids is on the edge of a development dilemma. At present it continues to lack the science base and resources to move forward. The reality of the petroleum situation is that replacement technologies will eventually be needed. The reality of the technology history is that the development of such replacement technologies will require a substantial effort. Such an effort appears to be beyond our institutional technical ability at this time. The reasons for this fact are not known and are in need of analysis.

In sum, the status of DCL as a technology is as follows:

- Discovery of the potential for DCL: 1920s–1930s
- Development of crude DCL plants in Europe (first-generation technology): 1930s–1940s
- Small-scale basic science support efforts in Europe and the United States: 1920s–1930s
- Demonstration of first-generation technologies in the United States: 1940s–1950s
- Development of second-generation technologies, by industry, with some small government support after 1961: 1950s–1973
- Crash development program with heavy government support for second-generation technologies: 1973–1982
- End of present technology cycle: 1982–1987

The result of this history is that DCL as a technology is an empirically proven concept that has been demonstrated at a first-generation level. Further attempts to develop the technology have resulted in a second generation of techniques that have at best (in the United States) been demonstrated at the pilot plant stage. By comparison, the modern computer in a time frame less than that associated with the development of DCL has evolved through five distinct evolutionary periods. Each of these periods have been based on the development of fundamental knowledge that enabled engineers designing new computer architectures to understand the fundamentals of the planned processes before designing the machines. Such has not been the case in the technology history of DCL. Engineers have approached the problem without a firm knowledge of the chemistry or structure of the principal feedstock material. This lack of knowledge has contributed to the poor design of both the first- and the second-generation technologies and more importantly has limited the evolutionary growth potential of DCL in total.

Our goals in this effort are to understand and explain the characteristics of the technology development environment surrounding DCL and from this explanation to understand better the potential and the barriers for future DCL developments. The two ensuing chapters detail our approach to this task.

2 —————————— *RETROSPECTIVE TECHNOLOGY ASSESSMENT: METHODS AND APPROACH*

INTRODUCTION

As a self-conscious and systematic enterprise, technology assessment is no more than twenty years old. The term itself seems to have emerged for the first time from the U.S. House of Representatives' Science and Astronautics Committee, specifically from a report issued by the Subcommittee on Research and Development. According to the chairman of the subcommittee,

Technology assessment is a form of policy research which provides a balanced appraisal to the policymaker. Ideally, it is a system to ask the right questions and obtain correct and timely answers. It identifies policy issues, assesses the impact of alternative courses of action and presents findings. It is a method of analysis that systematically appraises the nature, significance, and merit of technological progress.[1]

The definition given above is perhaps the earliest extant, but it is one that still provides a good description of the activities typically included under the technology assessment rubric. The definition is also useful in that it provides a marked distinction between technology assessment and traditional engineering-oriented studies focusing on technical feasibility or the technological state of the art. From its inception, technology assessment has included a concern with social and economic factors and a mission to provide information relevant to public-policy decision making.[2]

In many of its applications, technology assessment has been closely

13

associated with technological forecasting.[3] The affinity of the two approaches is clear. Typically each is concerned with the interaction of
technological and socioeconomic factors, each is concerned about estimating impacts, each relies on a wide array of traditional social sciences
and engineering-based analytical tools, and each tends to be anticipatory
in its perspective. The approach taken in this study differs from most
assessment/forecasting efforts in that the purposes are not primarily
anticipatory. The concern here is to provide a retrospective technology
assessment. While technological forecasting has often looked back,
chiefly as a means of validating forecasting techniques through retrodic-
tion,[4] technology assessment has had its eye on current and future impacts with little concern for retrospective analysis. Perhaps the limited
concern for retrospective technology assessment is best explained by its
genesis as a means of mitigating pressing social and economic problems
arising from technology.

Retrospective technology assessment (RTA) is a methodological invention of recent origin, little standardization, and infrequent application. The development of RTA seems to have been spurred by a National Science Foundation grant for a conference examining the uses of
historical methods in assessing technology. That conference yielded a
volume that is still the major theoretical work in RTA.[5] While no other
major theoretical–methodological compendia have been published since
that time, a handful of RTA applications have been undertaken.[6] Finally, a few journal articles have considered the merits of various approaches to RTA.[7] As matters stand, RTA is an approach whose potential remains largely untapped. This is especially the case in regard to its
applications as a technology policy analysis tool. The few RTAs that have
been undertaken have focused on events that transpired at least one
hundred years ago and are of much more interest to historians than to
persons involved in contemporary technology policy.

The chief purpose of this chapter is to provide a methodological perspective for the remainder of the study. This is accomplished in three
sections. Much of this analysis is similar to any traditional technology
assessment effort and, thus, a first section deals with some of the more
general methodological questions pertinent to technology assessment.
However, since this is a retrospective technology assessment, there are
also important respects in which the methods employed here differ from
technology assessments aimed at understanding current or future impacts and, thus, a second section deals with methodological issues specific to RTA. Finally, a third section of the chapter deals with methodological issues and approaches specific to this analysis. As mentioned,
previous RTAs have dealt with technological events that were chronolog-
ically far-removed. Since our effort emphasizes events occurring since
World War II, it is dissimilar in some respects from other RTAs. In

particular, the archival research task is not nearly as formidable for this analysis, but the policy research and economic analysis aspects are much more central, extensive, and challenging. In sum, the RTA undertaken here makes much more extensive use of analytical approaches common to professional policy analysis and, at least in that respect, resembles technological forecasting and anticipatory technology assessment more than the RTAs produced to date.

METHODOLOGICAL ISSUES IN TECHNOLOGY ASSESSMENT

The methodological issues involved in technology assessment are as complex and as controversial as one might expect given the multi-disciplinary nature of the enterprise. It is not our purpose in this section to deal with the full range of methodological issues associated with technology assessment.[8] While there is some attempt to provide a broad-based orientation, our focus is on those issues that seem particularly relevant to the overall objective of this analysis, namely, understanding the evolution of direct coal liquefaction technologies.

The issues most pertinent for us can be summarized in just a few basic questions, and these questions are used to organize the discussion presented in this section. The questions include:

1. What are the prerequisites for effective technology assessment?
2. What methods are available and what particular methods are most appropriate for understanding the evolution of direct coal liquefaction technologies?
3. How does one set boundaries on technology assessment?

On the assumption that at least some readers have limited familiarity with technology assessment, the first question includes some general background. However, the emphasis here as elsewhere is on issues that are germane to the current analysis.

What Are the Prerequisites for Effective Technology Assessment?

Technology assessment has been defined as "a class of policy studies which systematically examine the effects on society that may occur when a technology is introduced, extended or modified."[9] This definition has much in common with other familiar definitions such as Carpenter's description of technology assessment as "the process of technology taking a purposeful look at the consequences of technological change," a process that includes cost/benefit analyses but "goes beyond these to identify affected parties and unanticipated impacts in as broad and long range a fashion as is possible."[10]

These definitions provide a useful point of departure because they highlight some of the differences between the present study of direct coal liquefaction (DCL) and most technology assessments. The chief distinction of the technology assessment presented here is that the focus is less on the impact of the technologies on society than on the impact of socioeconomic factors, acting in concert with technical factors, on the development of the technologies. While most technology assessments recognize the possibilities for reciprocal effects, the focus is usually on the impact of the technology on external events rather than on the impact of external events on the development of the technology.

Returning to the question of the effectiveness of technology assessment, Porter and his associates have identified three broad concerns of technology assessment: (1) breadth; (2) validity; (3) utility.[11] Thus, technology assessment is distinguished from more traditional engineering studies by its breadth of concerns. Technology assessment tends to be holistic in its orientation. That is to say, the approach involves an effort to consider not just technological system elements but the technological system as a whole and the diverse interaction effects among its elements.[12] Furthermore, whereas much of traditional policy analysis focuses on one or a small set of effectiveness outcome variables, technology assessment is typically more interested in providing understanding of the workings of a complex sociotechnical system. In response to technology assessment's concerns with providing a holistic view and with mapping complexity, a variety of techniques have been developed to help measure and predict cross-impacts among key variables in the system.[13]

The validity of technology assessment is often a troublesome issue. One reason is that validity carries a number of connotations. The most common of these, perhaps, is the truth of propositions about causal relationships. The fact that there is sometimes no clear-cut distinction between independent and dependent variables compounds validity problems. However, validity remains a central objective in technology assessment.

Many traditional scientific standards are not appropriate for gauging the validity of technology assessment. In part this is because of the fact that holistic approaches are intermingled with analytical approaches more suitable for decomposition of systems. In part this is because technology assessment tends to be oriented to future conditions and anticipated effects, and no truly valid claims can be made about causal relationships among future states of affairs.[14] In retrospective technology assessment it is theoretically possible to employ data that permit causal

e to those conditions as a virtual black box? Or does one examine
tical factors involved? And if one does study causation at the level
le East politics, how deeply does one dig to determine the ulti-
fects of, say, the rise of OPEC on the somewhat far-removed
elated to the development of DCL technology? The challenge of
ry setting for technology assessment is that one walks a tightrope
the error of neglecting factors that are of critical causal impor-
nd the futility of dealing with events that are poorly understood
sely connected to the focal technologies. In sum, it is easy to see
many technology assessments rise or fall on early decisions estab-
boundaries.[26]

ite the difficulties inherent in the boundary-setting process for
ogy assessment, there are a few rules of thumb that can be identi-
rg[27] has discussed some of the factors to be taken into account in
ry setting for technology assessment. While his discussion is more
riate for anticipatory technology assessment than for RTA, some
guidelines can be adapted.

st concern is to bound the technology assessment in time. In an
atory TA this is usually done by the sponsor and is a function of
icy planning horizon. In the case of an RTA, however, the policy
ng horizon has little direct effect on the boundary setting process.
, the choice of time frame has more to do with the rate at which
hnology of interest has changed and the stages in the develop-
f the technology. In many instances, the RTA gives uneven treat-
o historical periods and stages of development of the technology,
ling on the importance of each stage to current and future
oments.

cond factor identified by Berg is the spatial dimension. Is the TA
to national boundaries, or regions, or institutions? This is often
ortant issue when policymakers sponsoring a TA are interested in
hting events occurring within their own jurisdiction. In the case
current analysis, it is useful to limit different aspects of the RTA to
nt spatial boundaries. Specifically, the technical developments of
ave occurred throughout the world and limiting attention only to
n the United States would be highly artificial and misleading.
er, it is reasonable to limit much of the assessment of public policy
onomic factors to U.S. boundaries because: (1) there is little lever-
policy change in other nations, and (2) the analysis becomes
y too complex if close scrutiny is given to international political
onomic issues.

latter boundary choice—that is, the focus on U.S. economic and
change—is consistent with another of Berg's rules of thumb, that
ost appropriate institutional focus is on those actors who have
d policy and remain important in the policy arena. Less clear-cut,
er, is boundary setting for what Berg calls "impact sectors," the

inference. However, in most instances events are studied in a particularistic fashion with methods more akin to history than science.[15]

Moreover, in RTA, validity revolves around two desiderata. First,
there is the traditional source of validity of studies employing historical
or ethnographic methods: the face validity of the source data. From this
perspective, a more valid RTA is one that employs high quality data
directly relevant to the issue at hand. A second kind of validity is more
closely related to the traditional validity questions of science. While it is
not often possible in RTA to employ sufficient control or rigor to make
strong cause–effect statements, it is possible to judge the "credibility
logic" of an analysis. While this approach is elaborated elsewhere,[16] its
elements can be outlined succinctly: First, provide an explicit statement
about the causal relationships inferred; second, provide a "credibility
logic" tracing the origins and rationales for those assumptions; third,
employ methods and assumptions that can be clearly adjudicated by
others.

Another approach to validity, one detailed in a subsequent section, is
more dialectical in its nature. If it is not possible, due to data limitations
or due to the interpretive nature of historical events, to develop consensus about causal relationships, it is often useful to take the very different
tack of systematically pitting arguments against one another. The assumption is that pitting alternative explanations against one another will
have the effect of winnowing arguments and permitting the strongest
explanation, often a synthesizing explanation, to emerge. Dialectical
methods have long been used in technological forecasting[17] and seem to
have equal promise for RTA.

Porter and associates' third criterion for technology assessment, utility,
is at the same time obvious and nettlesome. While it is easy to agree that
any technology assessment should meet the utility criterion, it is not an
easy matter to determine just what this means. Utility is an externally
defined criterion and is likely to vary from one person or party to the
next. However, Porter and associates do identify several elements of
utility, including (1) relevance, asking the question in such a manner that
the answer is of interest to the sponsor of the technology assessment; (2)
timeliness, the assessment should be ready when needed to inform policy
deliberation; (3) credibility, regardless of "objective" validity, the product must be viewed as credible by the sponsor; (4) communicability,
findings must be presented in a usable format.

In addition to the three broad effectiveness criteria mentioned by
Porter and associates, another comes to mind that is especially pertinent
to the present study. Effectiveness depends on the ability to harness an
interdisciplinary perspective. The interdisciplinary nature of technology
assessment is discussed at length in a number of sources,[18] some of

which provide prescriptions to enhance the effectiveness of multi-disciplinary teams.[19] The development of an interdisciplinary perspective is vital to the current analysis because of the broad mix of factors—scientific, technological, social, economic—and the multiplicity of analytical methods employed. This dictates an interdisciplinary approach and implies that the integration of approaches is central to the effectiveness of the assessment.[20]

What Technology Assessment Methods are Appropriate?

The broad outlines (meta-method) of technology assessment methodology have been presented in several studies. Before considering which particular methods are most appropriate to the problem of an RTA of direct coal liquefaction, it is useful to review some of the broad descriptions of technology assessment methodology. One of the first attempts to codify technology assessment methodology was undertaken by the National Academy of Engineering and resulted in the identification of sequential steps involved in technology assessment activity.[21] These sequential steps include:

1. Identify and refine the subject to be assessed;
2. Delineate the scope of the assessment and develop a data base;
3. Identify alternative strategies to solve the selected problems with the technology under assessment;
4. Identify parties affected by the selected problems and the technology;
5. Identify the impacts on the affected parties;
6. Valuate or measure the impacts;
7. Compare the pros and cons of alternative strategies.

While the NAE report was a useful first step, the first comprehensive attempt to outline a technology assessment methodology was presented in a report of the Mitre Corporation.[22] The method developed by Mitre served as a prototype and was applied in a variety of technology assessments in diverse fields including automotive emission reduction, computer networking, aquaculture, and industrial enzymes. The Mitre method involved seven major steps and, as in most technology assessments, viewed technology more as a cause than as an effect.

The pilot technology assessments undertaken by Mitre provided some initial lessons about the interaction among component variables. Relatedly, it became clear that the identification of sequential steps in technology assessment, while analytically convenient, masked the interactive nature of technology assessment.

The effort to build general methodologies for technology assessment

has been beneficial in many respects. In particula[...] of the Mitre researchers helped to codify a high[...] inquiry. However, it is important to note that (1) [...] methods should and do vary as a function of the s[...] (2) each technology assessment encounters uniq[...] and, as a result; (3) technology assessment meth[...] be) two parts ad hoc design to one part standard[...]

The technology assessment presented here is b[...] of Rossini, Porter, and Zucker,[24] as a "miniassess[...] roassessment considers the "full range of implica[...] sidered in depth,"[25] a miniassessment provides an[...] analysis, one that is more sharply bounded and v[...] are examined on a more limited basis.

One methodological feature of the current te[...] that it is a miniassessment and employs techniq[...] level of analysis. The choice of method is also sha[...] is a retrospective technology assessment. This [...] things, that historical and class methods are [...] While there are certain respects in which case [...] limited, it is possible to make good use of case-o[...] as one appreciates that case studies have their [...] contrast to technology assessments more oriente[...] sis, case studies provide richer insights into th[...] events and are more helpful in providing in-de[...] impact of particular policies and social and tec[...] depth is, of course, gained at a cost. What is lost [...] often afforded by quantitative analysis and, to so[...] ized approaches to measurement and evaluatic[...] quantitative technology assessment.

In sum, the fact that the current technology ass[...] implies that the choice of methods will be some[...] methods employed in anticipatory technology as[...] ular differences are elaborated in a subsequent [...]

What Is the Approach to Setting Boundaries[...]

Boundary setting is a vital element of any techn[...] is particularly crucial in a miniassessment exam[...] gies influenced by a great number of external [...] example, that Middle East politics has an impact [...] the price of oil, in turn, affects the economic attr[...] liquefaction, which, in turn, affects the developr[...] But knowing this, how does one set the bounda[...] one begin with the economic conditions and treat[...]

range of individuals affected by a technology or set of technologies. In the RTA we have defined impact sectors in a relatively narrow fashion and have, as indicated, devoted less attention to the impact of the technology on society than vice versa. To the extent that it makes sense to set boundaries for this study on impact sectors, the focus here is on government sponsors of energy research and on industrial actors who have or might in the future have an interest in the development of DCL.

Often the most difficult boundary to set is the scientific–technological boundary. In the case of the current RTA this problem is reduced somewhat by the focus on DCL as an example of synthetic fuels technology. There is another issue, however, that is not so easily resolved: the connection between coal science (and the many related sciences) and coal liquefaction technology. In general, there is much debate about the relationship between basic science and technological development and studies have indicated that the contribution of science to technological development is not straightforward and may be a function of the "embeddedness" of science. Since the present analysis is a miniassessment it will not be possible to set a broad boundary around the scientific knowledge base of coal liquefaction technology. As a rule of thumb, our analysis is limited to scientific studies aimed directly at enhancing knowledge of coal and contributing to the development of liquefaction. This is, of course, an important limitation since many of the most important current areas of liquefaction research draw from scientific areas seemingly far removed from coal research.

The boundary for the current study is expansive in some respects and narrow in others. Specifically, it is relatively narrow in respect to the technological focus and impact sector, but more expansive with respect to the time frame of the study and the spatial domain examined.

IMPLICATIONS OF RETROSPECTIVE TECHNOLOGY ASSESSMENT

The current technology assessment has many points in common with conventional anticipatory technology assessments, including, for example, the need to delimit the technology and other boundaries to the study, a commitment to holistic analysis of the impacts of technology, and an interest in studying indirect impacts as well as direct ones. However, the fact that the current analysis is an RTA has several important implications, many of which distinguish it from conventional TA.

How Does RTA Differ from Traditional TA?

The most obvious way in which RTA differs from traditional TA is its historical focus. The fact that RTA examines events in history, rather than current impacts of possible future impacts, provides some distinct advantages and disadvantages. RTA, unlike anticipatory TA, can rigorously test narrow gauge propositions. Events occurred or did not occur, trends can be tracked, universal propositions can be disconfirmed. None of this is possible in anticipatory TA. However, RTA has few advantages in imputing causality among events and in sorting out spurious associations from important, direct relationships.

Another important way in which RTA differs from conventional TA is in its paucity. Several hundred conventional technology assessments have been performed but only a handful of RTAs are reported in the literature. This means that any RTA must sort out methodological and design questions as it goes along for there is no standard, accepted RTA method. Indeed, there is not even a prototype "meta-method" of the type produced by the NAE and the Mitre Corporation. The success of an RTA depends greatly on the ability to make decisions about novel methodological issues.

RTA is distinct, and distinctly advantaged, in its ability to choose time frames according to tangible and valid criteria. In anticipatory TA the choice of time frame is, ultimately, an exercise in speculation. When will a technology come to fruition? When will its impacts be felt? What rate of change can be expected? What interaction effects are likely? All these factors are unknowable in anticipatory TA but in RTA there are usually empirical cues for making these demonstrations. It has been argued that one of the most important factors in the success of RTA is the ability to make decisions about the time lines for RTA and the relative emphasis to place on different periods in the life of the technology.[28] In RTA there are usually some tangible criteria for making those judgments.

How Does RTA Differ From Traditional History of Technology?

Much of the distinction between RTA and traditional TA flows directly from the historical orientation of RTA. But it is important to note that there are significant differences in orientation between RTA and conventional history of technology.[29]

Some of those differences can be succinctly summarized. RTA typically takes a "broader cut" than does history of technology. While it is true that history writ large often takes a sweeping view that sometimes encompasses whole epochs, history of technology tends to be focused on single technologies for relatively brief periods and sometimes considers the role of just a few or even a single actor. Typical titles include "Benjamin Hold and the Invention of the Track-Type Tractor,"[30] "Farish Furman's Formula: Scientific Farming and the New South,"[31] and "Applied Microscopy and American Park Diplomacy: Charles Wardell Stiles in Germany."[32] Despite admonitions to take broader and more interpretative views of history of technology,[33] most historians of technology have been reluctant to venture beyond description of narrow events.

One of the most important ways in which RTA differs from history of technology is in the use of systematic conceptual models. Historians are wont to avoid explanation, and in those instances where explanation accompanies description, historians provide explanations that are essentially akin to literary interpretation. By contrast, RTA practitioners employ conceptual models and other such devices in their identification of variables[34] and in specifying methods and approaches to inference.[35]

Historians of technology rarely provide explicit hypotheses and even more rarely hypotheses that are testable and refutable. By contrast, RTA succeeds or fails according to the ability of the analyst to provide plausible and testable hypotheses. This point is related to the previous one. Often the hypotheses provided in RTA flow from the conceptual model employed. Cases developed in RTA are selected in such a manner as to enable testing of hypotheses and according to variables chosen for analysis. In this respect the logic of inquiry for RTA is similar to that of systematic case study analysis.

WHAT IS DISTINCT ABOUT THE RETROSPECTIVE TECHNOLOGY ASSESSMENT OF DIRECT COAL LIQUEFACTION?

The specific details of the analytical methods and assumptions of this study are provided in a subsequent chapter. However, it is useful at this point to highlight some of the particulars of the design employed here.

An important assumption of this RTA is that valuable insights can be gained by considering the development of technology from the perspective of alternative models of development. The models employed here are, in a sense, elementary. Coal liquefaction is viewed, alternately, from the perspectives of an Economic Model, a Policy Model, a Technological Model, and a Synthesis Model. Roughly, the Economic Model assumes at the outset that the best explanation of the development of DCL is provided by analysis of economic factors and then sets out to marshall the best evidence for that elemental assumption. Likewise, the Policy Model has as its cardinal assumption that changes in public policy have been the most critical in determining the course of DCL and provides evidence supporting that view. According to the Technological Model, DCL is best explained by the rate and direction of progress in coal science and technical knowledge pertaining to DCL. Naturally, no one model gives a full account and, of course, the variables in the respective models are closely related in many instances. However, it is analytically useful to begin by separating explanations in order that a synthesizing explanation can be developed. Thus, the approach to inquiry is essentially dialectical: pitting one explanation against another in order to determine the merits of each and to help identify linkages among explanatory factors.

The method described above is employed at two different levels. It is used to describe the development of DCL, but it is also used in connection with one particular DCL technology: H-coal. The purpose of operating at these two different levels of analysis is to afford different perspectives: both a global and a particularistic perspective.

Another distinctive feature of this RTA is the aforementioned concentration on the impacts of external factors on the development of technology, rather than the more traditional (in TA) focus on the impact of the technology on society. This perspective simplifies matters in one respect. Most TAs must struggle with the question of setting boundaries on second and higher order effects. But here we are chiefly interested in direct effects: the factors affecting the development of DCL.

An important part of the methodology for this RTA is the "interviewing" of data sources, a method described and advocated by Hamilton.[36] For each of the models employed here (excepting only the Synthesis Model), a questionnaire is developed that is intended to guide not only the actual interviews but also examination of secondary data sources. In describing this technique, Hamilton observes that "the questionnaire must be formulated to allow a systematic analysis of the data without limiting the researcher's ability to discover anomalies or unexpected patterns."[37] This technique is more fully described in a subsequent chapter.

3 —————— ANALYTICAL FRAMEWORK FOR RETROSPECTIVE TECHNOLOGY ASSESSMENT OF DIRECT COAL LIQUEFACTION

The foregoing chapter has provided a backdrop for this chapter's discussion of the specific analytical framework employed in this retrospective technology assessment.

In Chapter 2 a brief overview of RTA was presented, including a general discussion of technology assessment and its methods, an account of the differences between traditional TA and RTA, and a brief explanation of the ways in which the present particular RTA is distinctive. This chapter elaborates on the methods employed in this RTA of direct coal liquefaction technology.

There are four related analytical processes employed in the RTA. The first of these, "interviewing the data," is a means of placing structure on what is essentially a qualitative analysis. The second, "model development," employs a variant of the dialectical method to arrive at the most comprehensive explanation of the development of DCL. The third, analysis of a "base-line case," provides detail and context against which to compare the broader analysis of DCL. Finally, "validation processes" are described. Each of these analytical processes is discussed in turn. In a concluding section of this chapter there is a discussion of the steps required for developing a synthesis from diverse explanatory models.

INTERVIEWING THE DATA: AN APPROACH TO QUALITATIVE ANALYSIS

In one of the few existing works detailing the RTA methodology, Mary Hamilton suggests a seven step approach to RTA. Those seven steps include:

1. The technology and the context of the technology development are defined.
2. Based on those definitions, data sources are identified.
3. A questionnaire to "interview" the data sources is formulated and applied.
4. Based on the results of applying the questionnaire, a "standard development case" is applied.
5. Notable exceptions to aspects of the standard development case are identified, described, and documented, and the conditions under which they occurred are described.
6. If there are sufficient notable exceptions, one or more alternative development cases are developed.
7. A "standard baseline" (nondevelopment) case is formulated by means of the same questionnaire approach.[1]

This analysis employs some of the methodological procedures outlined by Hamilton, but not all the steps are taken here and approaches not discussed by Hamilton are applied in their stead. The two most relevant aspects of the approach outlined by Hamilton are "interviewing the data" and development of a "standard baseline case." The latter step is discussed in a subsequent section of this chapter.

The information sources from which the research chapters draw are extremely diverse, including interviews, government documents, historical accounts, and analysis of aggregate data. This fragmented information is not easily digested. As a tool for helping to organize the information and assimilate it as a database for the models employed in the RTA, the technique of interviewing the data is employed. Essentially, this involves specification of a questionnaire, followed by distillation of the data in answer to the questions on questionnaire. The formal elaboration of the questionnaire items acts to force some discipline on the qualitative analysis and guides the research. The approach is also fundamental to development of hypotheses and identification of variables of interest.

The primary data source for this analysis was expert opinion. To this end a panel of experts was developed and this panel provided insights that could not otherwise have been attained. The object of forming the panel was to thoroughly review the history, the evolution of first- and second-generation processes, the present state of the art, the significance of science and engineering in the development, and the policy and political action environment in which DCL has evolved in the United States.

The panel was interviewed in person or by telephone using one of two different interview protocols. The two protocols are presented in Appendixes 1 and 2. The interviewees were assured that direct quotes would not be used in any publications resulting from the interview. In cases where direct quotes could be traced directly to one of the respondents, they were assured that a paraphrase of the quote would be used. They were also assured that references to particular corporate activities would be protected.

The expert panel included the following persons:

Name	Position	Organization
Dwain Spencer	V.P. & Dir. of Advanced Power Systems Division	Electric Power Research Institute
Martin Gorbaty	Scientific Coordinator	Exxon Research & Engineering Co.
Robert Epperly	V.P. of Research & Development	Fueltech Inc.
A. G. Comolli	Manager, Coal Liquefaction	Hydrocarbon Research Inc.
J. B. McLean	Senior Process Development Expert	Hydrocarbon Research Inc.
Marvin Greene	Manager of Process Development	Lummus Crest Inc.
David Gray	Dept. Staff, Energy Resource & Environmental Systems Division	Mitre Corporation
Glen Tomlinson	Dept. Staff, System Planning & Analysis	Mitre Corporation
D. Duayne Whitehurst	Research Scientist	Mobil Research & Development Co.
Thomas W. Johnson	Research Engineer	Southern Company Services, Inc.
Gary A. Styles	Research Program Supervisor, Fuel Processing Programs	Southern Company Services, Inc.
George Hill	EIMCO Professor, Dept. of Chemical Engineering	University of Utah (Former OCR Director)
Douglas Keller	V.P. of Technology	Otisca Industries

THREE MODELS FOR EXPLAINING DCL

Each of the three models employed here begins with a basic axiomatic assumption. The *technology model* assumes that the development of DCL is best explained by scientific and technological change with significant external influence; the *economic model* assumes that DCL development is best accounted for by DCL, and that other factors can be treated as irrelevant; the *policy model* assumes that DCL development is a function

Table 3.1.
Interview Schedule for Economic Model of DCL Development

The objective of this questionnaire is to identify the most significant economic variables pertaining to DCL development and to provide information, obtained from diverse sources, about the form and direction of relationships among those variables. Generally, each of these questions is applied for a variety of time frames.

Q1   What is the division of costs between basic research, applied research, development, demonstration?

Q2   Who bears the cost? What tax incentives are available to industry to reduce costs? What financial instruments are available?

Q3   What mechanisms, legal, financial, industry-specific, are available to ensure appropriability of industrial R&D investments?

Q4   Who bears the cost of failure of development?

Q5   What are appropriate measures of economic "success" in development? Are there notable examples of economic "successes" and "failures"?

Q6   What is the projected price per barrel of liquid fuel? How does that compare with the price of oil and other conventional energy sources?

Q7   What has been the trend of the price of oil in the previous 6 months?

Q8   What percentage of U.S. oil consumption was derived from imports?

Q9   What was the rate of patent issuance in areas directly related to DCL development?

Q10   What was the rate of exploration and well drilling among U.S. producers?

Q11   What is the estimate of risk associated with investment in synthetic fuels in general? in DCL?

Q12   What was the position of the "analytical group" at the American Petroleum Institute?

Q13   What was the status of government incentives for investment?

Q14   What was the level of concentration and vertical integration in the U.S. oil industry?

Q15   What was the perception of potential for possible supply interruption?

of politics and public policy and that economic and technical factors are subsidiary.

The purpose of this approach is to take advantage of the insights that often emerge from dialectical inquiry. The basic idea of directing technology assessment according to multiple models has been discussed by Bozeman and Rossini.[2] It is assumed that by strongly arguing for one perspective and then another on the development of events, a clearer picture is presented and a synthesis may be produced that takes on elements of each explanation.[3] This synthesis is presented in the conclusion for this report. In constructing each of the models, a guiding questionnaire is used to "interview the data." These guidepost questions are presented below.

"Interviewing the Data": The Economic Model Questionnaire

To reiterate, the *economic model* begins with the assumption that economic variables provide the most effective explanation of DCL development and, for the most part, the boundaries of the RTA are limited to domestic economic factors. Naturally, domestic economic factors cannot be understood in a vacuum, but as a matter of emphasis international economic factors are treated in a less detailed fashion. Table 3.1 provides the preliminary questionnaire for "interviewing the data" pertaining to the economic model.

"Interviewing the Data": The Policy Model Questionnaire

While many of the issues of politics and public policy are, from a practical standpoint, inseparable from economic variables, it is useful from an analytical perspective to seek a set of policy questions that are at least partly distinct. The policy questions are presented in Table 3.2. Again, the presumption of the policy model is that political and public policy factors present the most trenchant explanation of DCL development in the United States.

"Interviewing the Data": The Technology Model Questionnaire

The *technology model* assumes that socioeconomic variables are of limited significance in DCL development and that the best explanation comes from an understanding of the scientific and technical dimensions of DCL. Table 3.3 gives the questions used in construction of the technology model.

Table 3.2.
Interview Schedule for the Public Policy Model of DCL Development

Q1   What was the policy perspective of the national administration in power toward federal involvement in industrial development?

Q2   What was the position of the API, NCA, and other interest groups toward synthetic fuels? toward DCL?

Q3   What was the political distribution of the "coal state" senators and representatives in the key interior and later energy related sub-governments?

Q4   What was the trend in coal consumption in the previous 5–10 years?

Q5   What was the government's annual budget for research? for coal research?

Q6   What were the major pieces of legislation related to CL recently passed at the federal level?

Q7   What was the trend in consumer energy prices in the previous 12–24 months?

Q8   What was the perceived probability of energy supply cutoffs or shortages? price increases?

Q9   What was the relative importance of energy policy on the national agenda?

Q10   What party controlled the House? the Senate? the White House?

Q11   What was the perception of international competition for development of CL?

Q12   What was the linkage between demonstration project siting or research location and congressional committee membership?

Q13   What was the percentage of oil demand filled by imports? What was the perception of the geographic distribution of those percentages?

Q14   What companies supported the development of DCL technologies? What was their rationale?

Q15   What was the general trend of the U.S. Congress in funding coal related research?

Q16   What was the general trend of the national administration in requesting funding for coal research?

Q17   What companies had the largest coal research efforts? Did they support coal research activities?

Q18   What was the level of legislative debate surrounding DCL at the federal level?

Q19   What was the perceived level of technical risk associated with DCL technology options (agency, congress, industry)?

Q20   What was the political strength associated with the various DCL options? with DCL in general?

Q21   What was the level of interest in DCL by the defense establishment?

Q22   To what extent was liquefaction technology development linked to national defense?

Table 3.3.
Interview Schedule for Technology Model of DCL Development

Q1   What major breakthroughs occurred in DCL technology in the previous five years?

Q2   What was the patent rate in areas related to DCL in the previous 2 years?

Q3   What were the major technical barriers to DCL (in rank order)?

Q4   Who were the major technology development groups involved in DCL?

Q5   Who were the major scientific groups supporting DCL development efforts?

Q6   What were the conversion effects of the leading processes?

Q7   What was the potential for leading processes to produce quality fuels and chemical feedstocks?

Q8   What were the longest run times of various DCL options at the PDU scale? pp scale? demo scale?

Q9   What were the (perceived) time frames associated with commercialization of the various DCL options in the query year?

Q10   What were the major operating problems associated with each of the DCL options?

Q11   What was the flexibility of each DCL option with regard to variation in coal feedstock?

Q12   What was the state of knowledge regarding coal chemistry and structure?

Q13   What major developments would reduce the cost of DCL?

Q14   To what extent and in what ways did U.S. R&D add to the first generation German technology? What were the generational heritage and status of the various U.S. options?

Q15   What were the technical limits of each viable option—production capacity, input requirements, output configurations? To what extent did the output configuration address the energy/fuel needs of the market?

Q16   To what extent was each of the viable processes designed on empirical or theoretical knowledge?

Q17   Was the concentration of science/technical resources devoted to DCL sufficient to provide a critical mass of activity in the field?

Q18   To what extent was knowledge regarding DCL development publicly available?

Q19   What key types or bits of scientific knowledge would have been most useful for development?

Q20   What was the perception of viability for DCL as a synthetic fuel option?

Q21   What was the concentration of DCL patents among major firms? the government?

Q22   What was the rate and direction of licensing?

THE BASELINE CASE: H-COAL

In this context, the purpose of the baseline case is to apply an implicit comparison throughout the study. H-Coal is chosen as the baseline case in part because it is a paradigmatic illustration of the major economic, technological, and policy issues in DCL. The objectives of doing so are (1) to provide, in a sense, through detail another level of analysis; (2) to calibrate the model by taking a more microscopic perspective.

Another reason for choosing H-Coal as a baseline case is less a function of method than the role of H-Coal in the recent history of DCL in the United States. H-Coal is, in many respects, a "morality tale" with implications for investments in DCL. H-Coal can be described as a technology that was (1) well supported for a period of time, (2) demonstrated as technologically viable, and (3) ultimately, put on the shelf. Much of the history of DCL development conforms to that three-step description, and much of this analysis is about the difficulties of going from a viable technology to marketable technology.

The Baseline Case as Another "Level of Analysis"

As a broader perspective is adopted, there is a better chance to develop generalizations, but there is also, perforce, a reduced role for circumstance and idiosyncrasy. Most of the RTA proceeds at a broad level and searches for generalizations and testable hypotheses. By considering at least one case, H-Coal, in greater detail than the other cases, it is possible to, in a sense, provide a different level of analysis, one more attuned to the role of idiosyncratic events. By taking this approach it is not only possible to get a more in-depth understanding of the development of H-Coal, but it is also possible to suggest the kinds of insights that are gained (and perhaps, the generalizations lost) had all the technologies been considered from a less broad perspective.

The Baseline Case as a Means of Calibration

In the development of measures it is sometimes useful to disaggregate in order to ensure that the broader measures one has constructed make sense when decomposed. For example, in developing a job satisfaction measure that is more global, one might wish to calibrate that measure by asking more detailed questions about satisfaction with task, co-workers, remuneration, and so forth and to determine whether the aggregation of those measures yields results similar to those obtained for the global measure. Much the same logic can be applied to calibration of models. Thus the baseline case considers in much greater detail all of the questions raised in the various "interview schedules" for the respective models.

To illustrate, let us consider the question in the economic model regarding the appropriability of returns on investment in R&D. Clearly one of the issues of appropriability is the protective benefits of patents. But whereas the more general analysis only goes so far as to stipulate the general provisions of patent laws and their impacts at various points in time, the more detailed baseline analysis for H-Coal goes much further and examines particular patents, cases designed to break patents, the role of particular patents vis-à-vis the use of trade secrets, and so forth. The assumption, then, is that the more general conclusions about the effects of patent changes on appropriability of R&D investment should conform to findings of the more detailed analysis. If there is little divergence, the model can be said to have been calibrated.

Finally, and not unimportantly, developing a baseline case provides an instance for comparison. An essentially qualitative analysis does not permit statistical comparisons across technologies and a rigid pair-wise comparison provides too much detail. By housing a single, familiar technology as a point of comparison, a conceptual benchwork is established.

VALIDITY ISSUES IN QUALITATIVE ANALYSIS

While the analyses presented in this RTA are systematic and the study seeks generalizations, the methods employed are much closer to history than to conventional science or even conventional technology assessment. This does not, however, lessen the concern with validity. Quite the reverse; the fact that the study is essentially qualitative requires not only a particular vigilance about validity but also requires multiple approaches to ensuring validity. In this study, validity is viewed as a function of four primary factors: (1) quality of data; (2) the nature of the test of hypotheses; (3) (previously mentioned) validation through comparison with a baseline case; (4) validation through dialectical processes. Each of these is discussed in turn.

Quality of the Data

Ensuring the quality of the data is a major concern in any systematic study, whether historical, prognostic, or traditionally scientific. If the data are inadequate the findings flowing from analysis of the data (no matter how rigorous the methods applied and no matter how tight the logic of analysis) are of limited value.

The primary technique for assuring the quality of the data involves taking care to seek out multiple sources. This is particularly important when the data come from interviews or private records. In the case of data in the public domain, multiple sources remain desirable. One might assume that public domain data, particularly widely available energy production and use statistics, would present few problems, because of the scrutiny undergone by multiple users. However, most users are not "data critical" and tend to take for granted the accuracy and precision of data.[4] As a general rule of thumb, this study will seek to have a minimum of two data sources. The researchers will, where appropriate, provide a commentary regarding their views of the quality of the data obtained for any part of the analysis.

The Nature of the Test of Hypotheses

The "interview schedules" presented in connection with each of the interpretative models—economic, policy, technological—provide implicit hypotheses. After the data required for those questions are obtained, formal hypotheses will be stated and evidence will be gathered for each of the hypotheses. Two types of hypotheses will be presented. In every case, it will be a requirement that the hypotheses presented are, at least in principle and as a matter of form, testable.

The first type of hypotheses, "broad gauge" hypotheses, will not be amenable to verification by the essentially historical methods employed in this RTA. This does not mean that broad gauge hypotheses are of no interest; quite the contrary. It simply means that inferences about the more basic and elemental causal factors will have to be treated with caution and that evidence will be viewed as a basis for interpretation more than as an anchor for well grounded explanation.

"Narrow gauge" hypotheses will in many cases be amenable to direct test. If the hypothesis deals with the particular behaviors of particular individuals or with the occurrence of events that can be documented, it will be possible to verify hypotheses. By the same token, it will be possible to falsify any universal proposition (e.g., a 5 percent or greater decrease in the price of oil always leads to a reduced demand for H-Coal) simply by uncovering a counter-instance.

Finally, it is worth noting that the most important element of rigor for any qualitative study is simply a concern with identifying testable hypotheses, regardless of the method of test.

Validation with a Baseline Case

The methodological uses of the baseline case have already been discussed above. Suffice it to say, the baseline validation, when taken with the requirement for multiple data sources, can be viewed as a dimensional matrix, with one dimension complementing the other. The requirement for multiple data sources can be viewed as a check on the reliability of data (the reliability of source or coding), whereas validation via the baseline case can be viewed as a check on the lens through which the data are examined.

Dialectical Processes

From Socrates through Hegel and to the present time, a central assumption of dialectical processes is that truth emerges from pitting opposition views against one another. Recently there has been much interest in the use of dialectical processes for policy analysis, planning, and strategic management[5] and approaches have been developed that compare dialectical inquiry and validation with other approaches. In this analysis, the dialectical process will be guided by the following steps to validation:

1. Logical inconsistencies among arguments (models) will be identified.
2. Empirical inconsistencies will be identified.
3. Empirical differences (not necessarily entailing inconsistencies) will be identified.
4. The evidence for respective logically inconsistent arguments will be carefully weighed; one argument will be accepted, the other rejected.
5. The evidence for empirical inconsistencies will be weighed. When two or more empirical inconsistencies still seem plausible after the evidence is weighed, the researchers will take one of three courses: (a) accept the most plausible empirical explanation, rejecting the others; (b) if possible, resolve inconsistencies through additional data collection or formulation of bridge principles[6]; (c) assign subjective probabilities to still inconsistent oppositions.
6. Provide explanations of differences among empirical propositions, seek to resolve differences via bridge principles or limiting the range of propositions.

As a result of the exercises in data validation, it will be possible to provide an explanatory framework that will enumerate propositions and express the form and degree of relationship among them. This is, of course, the rudimentary beginning of an informal theory and will serve as the grist for the conclusion of the study.

4 —————————————— PRE-1939 DEVELOPMENT OF DIRECT COAL LIQUEFACTION

Before one can go very far with the history of direct coal liquefaction, a few simple definitions are necessary. Direct coal liquefaction (DCL) is part of a general technological area called synthetic fuels. Synthetic fuel production starts with abundant but complex natural solid materials such as coal, peat, lignite, tar sands, or oil shale, which are all complex mixtures of organic molecules and mineral matter. Typically, mechanical methods can be used to separate much of the organic and mineral matter but the organic structure will also be contaminated with atomic elements that are common constituents of inorganic or mineral matter. These so-called "heteroatoms" include particularly nitrogen, oxygen, and sulfur. Their inclusion in the organic matter of these natural materials is a major factor in the complexity of synthetic fuel production.

From this point let us restrict all future discussion to coal, and in particular to bituminous and sub-bituminous coals. This restriction leads to a great narrowing of the discussion of synthetic fuel production and is also representative of the generic manner in which synthetic fuel development has occurred.

Starting with coal, the development of synthetic fuels derived from this natural material has evolved along two different technological lines. The first, direct coal liquefaction (DCL), involves turning the organic portions of the coal into a liquid at room temperature. The second technology involves the gasification of the organic matter in the coal to produce chiefly carbon monoxide (CO) and hydrogen (H_2). These gases are subsequently used as raw materials to synthesize gaseous and liquid hydrocarbon fuels in a process described as indirect coal liquefaction

(IDCL). The intermediate step in this process, coal gasification, has become a distinct technology leading to either the production of a low sulfur fuel suitable for electrical power production or as a raw material for producing a high Btu (British thermal unit) pipeline fuel.

The U.S. Office of Technology Assessment (OTA) in its 1982 report refers to synfuels production as a logical extension of current trends in oil refining. The report states: "As sources of the more easily refined crude oils are being depleted refiners are turning to heavier oils and tar sands. Oil shale and coal as starting materials for liquid hydrocarbon production are extreme cases of this trend to heavier feed stocks."[1] It is difficult for the present authors to accept this extreme as a logical extension of current practice and, as will be discussed, to date, so do oil refiners.

One major technological block to the ready production of synthetic fuels, the presence of the heteroatoms in the organic portion of the coal, has already been mentioned. But there is a more significant and fundamental block and that is the difference in hydrogen content in hydrocarbon fuels and in coal. The hydrogen content of coal will vary from a low of about 0.5 to 1.1 hydrogen atoms to 1 carbon atom in the organic portion of the coal. On the other hand, hydrocarbon gases and fuels will exhibit a variation in hydrogen content from a low of about 1.8 to a high of 4 hydrogen atoms to 1 carbon atom. Thus, there is a hydrogen deficit to make up in synthesizing fuel gases and liquids from coal. Ultimately, the cost of the hydrogen source to make up this deficit will control the cost and economic viability of direct coal liquefaction.

THE PRE-SCIENTIFIC ROOTS OF DCL

The following is a simple time line (see Fig. 4.1) tracing the early historical development of synthetic fuels based on coal. Today there is some controversy regarding development of coal liquefaction as to whether its development has been retarded by the lack of scientific development. Someone studying the early history of chemistry as an academic subject would find that allegation somewhat difficult to accept, in that coal and its derivatives were the subject of the development of much early chemical science.

By 1718 coke was being used in the production of iron from iron ore in blast furnaces. As many youngsters with a "Gilbert Chemistry Set" have learned, small bits of coal placed in a stoppered test tube fitted with a glass tube to allow gases to escape, will produce a gas that will readily burn and a black, charcoal-like porous residue. Much like charcoal, the porous residue or coke can be used as a smokeless household or industrial fuel but, of course, the major use of coke in the past has been in the reduction of iron ore in blast furnaces.

Figure 4.1.
Early Timelines in Synthetic Fuel from Coal Development

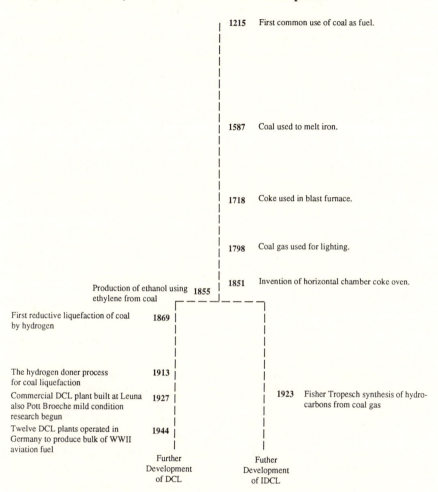

In 1855 Bertholet absorbed ethylene from coal gas in concentrated sulfuric acid and diluted and distilled the solution to recover the acid and produce ethyl alcohol. This process was the subject of a potential industrial development in France in 1862 on the basis that synthetic alcohol could be produced from coal at 30 percent of the cost of ethanol produced by fermentation.

In the process of producing metallurgical coke by heating coal to between 170 and 550°C, a ton of coal will produce about 1500 lbs. of coke, 10 gallons of tar, and 1000 cubic feet of coal gas. In the nineteenth century, as coke replaced charcoal in smelting iron, coke was made by charring the coal in open heaps. Later it was distilled in retorts to recover the coal tar that was in demand to replace wood gums that were becoming too expensive for commercial use. Murdock, an associate of James Watt, conceived of burning the previously wasted coal gas. This was the first commercial utilization of the scientific principle that had initiated the "great pneumatic revolution in chemistry."[2] An extensive treatment of the science and practice of coal gas (town gas) manufacture is provided by W. Richards.[3] This 1877 document provides great insight into the state of chemistry at that time as well as into its history.

The gas produced by the destructive distillation, carbonization, and pyrolysis, or coking, of coal will vary as a batch of coal is decomposed; but looking at the total volume of gas produced, it is mainly hydrogen and methane in about equal volumes, contaminated with ammonia, benzene, carbon dioxide, carbon monoxide, cyanide, cyanogen, cyclopentadiene, ethane, ethylene, hydrogen, hydrogen sulfide, naphthalene, nitric oxide, toluene, and water vapor. The volatile hydrocarbons can be recovered from the gas by scrubbing with a high-boiling-point oil. Thus coke oven gas provided a large number of chemical compounds that were extremely significant for the development of both a theoretical basis for chemical science and, on a practical basis, a gas that could be used as a source of heat and light.

The tar produced in the coking process was similarly a significant source of chemical species. Over 150 chemical compounds have been isolated, with naphthalene being the first in 1820 while the last 79 were not isolated until the period from 1931 to 1940.

Three classes of materials are present: (1) neutral hydrocarbons; (2) tar acids; and (3) tar bases. The wide variety of chemicals led to years of study attempting to identify the structure of these materials, their chemistry and potential applications. Efforts to separate the constituents of coal and coal tar led to developments in separation by distillation, polymerization, crystallization, and sublimation, or by putting acids or bases in solution as salts followed by neutralization to liberate the organic acid or base. Thus, much of the early science of inorganic, organic, and physical chemistry was built around destructive distillation of coal.

In addition, significant industries developed, including coke production, town gas production, and the distribution and manufacture of dyes and pharmaceuticals (the sulfa drugs among many others). The first dyes were produced from coal tar in 1834 but the effort continued over the next seventy years to produce a great variety of analine and azo based dyes. The synthetic coal tar dye industry first developed in Great Britain about 1870, but gradually the industry was transferred to and controlled by Germany. By 1913 Germany produced 75 percent of the dyes used in the Western industrial nations. In WWI the German dye patents were expropriated and licensed to Allied and U.S. firms that have subsequently grown to become among the world's largest corporations.

Chemists who were attracted to the study of the separation and analysis of the constituents of coal gas and tars became some of the most important contributors to this science. They included M. Berthelot, E. Fischer, W. H. Perkin, F. Runge, A. H. Hoffman, and C. Graebe among others.

With all the significance of coal and its derivatives to science and industry, very little scientific interest was directed to the basic structure and chemistry of the raw material. To some extent, the ease with which commercially valuable and scientifically significant compounds could be extracted from the coal mitigated against interest in the raw material. It seemed to indicate that with slightly harsher conditions the entire structure of the coal could be broken down. In the late 1800s and early 1900s—with significant markets for intact coal and coke, and with abundant sources of petroleum and natural gas available to supply the initially small markets for liquid fuels—there was no interest in another source of liquid hydrocarbons. But by about 1920 Europeans and even some in the United States began to be concerned by the rapid rate at which petroleum was being consumed. To some extent, the manner in which petroleum reserves were described (sufficient reserves for "X" years at the present rate of consumption) produced concern of a future shortage. This type of statement did not take into account what new reserves would be discovered in the meantime, and hence this approach was subsequently replaced by the discovery-rate technique, which examines the rate at which new reserves are added. By 1920, however, serious attention was being directed to the possibility of future petroleum shortages and the role coal could play in relieving such shortages.[4] This was particularly true in Germany, which suffered from a shortage of indigenous petroleum resources.

EARLY EXPERIENCE IN DCL

The first documented hydrogenation of coal was performed by Berthelot, as described in an 1869 article in the *Bulletin de la Société Chimique*.[5] The next reported work was that of Bergius in 1913, which led to a continuing effort by German chemical firms, with government support, to develop a liquid fuel capability using brown coal as the raw material. In 1925 Pier produced a motor fuel mixture from coal in a bench-scale apparatus. By September 1926, however, a plan to construct a 100,000 ton per day processing plant at Leuna was announced. This plant, completed in 1927, was plagued with technical difficulties and cost overruns. Production never reached more than 70,000 tons per day and by 1929 the developers, I. G. Farben, considered the product to be too expensive to be commercial. It was believed that additional R&D was needed before moving ahead with additional commercial production. Despite these arguments, however, the synthetic fuel effort continued as a means of developing raw materials to aid in the balance of payments problem Germany faced at the time.

The 1930–1945 German hydrogenation plants used hydrogen produced from coal by gasification. The carbon monoxide in the coal gas was converted to H_2 with the shift reaction and the resulting CO_2 was absorbed out. The purified hydrogen gas was delivered at pressures from 250 to 700 atm (3550 to 9940 psia).

The dried coal was pulverized and added to an approximately equal weight of a process-derived heavy oil, along with an iron or other more sophisticated catalyst (about one percent by weight) to form a paste.[6] The paste was injected into a five-foot diameter, one-foot long, heavy, cast, high-chrome steel hydrogenation forging with hydraulically operated ram pumps producing a pressure from 250 to 700 atm, depending on the plant. The hydrogen was preheated and then mixed with the paste in the hydrogenation units, which were maintained at the reaction temperature of 450°C. The hydrogen-to-oil ratio was 2000 m^3 to 1 ton of paste. Additional cold hydrogen was injected into the converters to control the temperature of the exothermic reaction and thus the yield of the reaction. Following reaction in the converter units, the products were separated into gas and liquid plus entrained solids phases in the so-called hot catch pot. The synthetic oil was entrained in the unreacted hydrogen as a vapor. The gas phase was cooled in a heat exchanger and the oil separated in the cold catch pot while the hydrogen was recycled. The oil product was reduced in pressure through let-down valves out of the cold catch pot and then distilled to separate motor fuels and middle oils, which were then further hydrogenated.

The heavy product (oil plus suspended solids) from the hot catch pot was also pressure reduced through let-down valves. The heavy oils were recycled to the pasting mill while the residual heavy oil that could not be filtered off from the suspended unreacted coal, mineral matter, and catalyst was pumped to a carbonization kiln. The heavy oil boiled off in the kiln was recycled while the coke residue (about 40 percent of the original coal) was dumped as a waste.

As German experience with hydrogenation grew, the operating pressures in the plants were increased in each successive plant. The operating pressure at Leuna was 200 atm (2840 psia). In the first bituminous coal plant at Scholyen (operational in 1939) the hydrogen pressure was increased to 300 atm (4260 psia). In the latest plants, built in 1943, it had increased to 700 atm (9940 psia). It was claimed that additional yield was obtained but it is not clear at what cost.

It was the conclusion of the British Ministry of Fuel and Power that the 1930 to 1944 German development of synthetic oil production was motivated purely by a desire for self-sufficiency in view of Nazi Germany's war purposes. The development of the synthetic fuel capability was not motivated by a "technical advance" or "economic justification."[7] Costs were entirely uneconomic compared with natural petroleum. As the Ministry goes on to note, the price of motor fuel from the Leuna plant, operating on extremely cheap brown coal, was double the cost of similar-quality imported fuel, without allowing for any margin of profit. Costs when operating on bituminous coal were even higher.

The process practiced in Germany up to 1945 was far from technically satisfactory. Erosion of pipe elbows, pump casings, and parts and let-down valves was extremely rapid. Most of the material used in building the plants, because of the high temperature and high hydrogen pressure, was necessarily high chrome (high cost) alloy steel. In the removal of inorganic wastes from the system, inevitably product was lost. One observation by the Ministry was particularly significant, considering the direction that DCL is taking forty-three years later: "The demonstration in the Bechhammer plant that coal could be converted at 700 atm into a product consisting mainly of asphalt-free heavy oil is of considerable interest in that it opens up the possibility of a two-stage liquid phase process for coal treatment, which would be expected to give about a 5 percent higher yield of petrol than processes used at present. Such improvement is not nearly sufficient, however, to alter the economic picture of coal hydrogenation at the existing level of coal and petrol prices." Thus, the advantage of two-stage liquefaction was in part recognized nearly forty-two years ago.

Was DCL successfully applied in Germany during WWII? German planes flew, and their armor moved. No one, to our knowledge, has made a successful case that Hitler's Germany was doomed by a lack of fuels and all the Allies had to do was sit back and wait for the German war machine to grind down to its inevitable end (a case that had been made with regard to Japan). In fact, quite the opposite was true. It was felt necessary to capture German territory to shut down their war potential including the development of new super weapons (jet aircraft, rockets, and the atom bomb).[8] Certainly WWII Germany had a fuel problem, but it was not crippling until the late stages of the war.

By that measure DCL enjoyed some success. By another measure, the adoption of German DCL technology by the WWII winners, it was a failure. German DCL technology was extensively evaluated both in terms of the technology and its economics, and it failed to win adoption by either the Western democracies or the Eastern bloc. The technical basis of that failure will now be explored from an American point of view.

FACTORS LIMITING THE SUCCESS OF DCL

The history of DCL through WWII was sufficient to reveal the major technical barriers to successful development. Two of these barriers have already been discussed briefly: (1) the difference in hydrogen content between the raw materials and the desired products, and (2) the need to remove the heteroatoms—oxygen, nitrogen, and sulfur—to prevent their incorporation in the products. Two other major barriers can be cited: (1) the mineralogy of coal; and (2) the chemical nature of coal. These are reviewed briefly below.

The Mineralogy of Coal

Coal as a mineral is ill defined, changing physically and chemically from micro-volume to macro-volume in the earth. Also, after removal from the earth it changes with time after it is mined. As the material is exposed to air, oxygen in the air oxidizes or otherwise chemically changes the constituents of the coal. Physically, the coal changes with time as water evaporates, the porosity degrades, and the structure collapses.

Much effort has been and is being devoted to a structural chemical definition of coal. Until the last ten years, coal both chemically and physically was ill defined. Today that picture is much improved. We now have chemical models that provide an average picture of the chemical constituents. We have physical models that describe the average structure of the material in terms of rank and maceral makeup. But again these are average descriptions and one must keep in mind the variation in chemical constituents and precise physical structure changes from micro-volume to macro-volume.

By its very nature coal is a heterogeneous material. Basically, it is natural vegetation debris that, with geologic time lapses, temperature, and sometimes pressure, has undergone a gradual transformation into peat, lignite (brown coal), bituminous coal, and anthracite. The mineral or in this case petrographic constituents, called macerals, have been classed as three main types. The organic portion of the coal consists essentially of carbon, hydrogen, and oxygen, with lesser amounts of sulfur and nitrogen. The organic matrix, however, is interrupted with inclusions of inorganic ash forming compounds (dirt) distributed as distinct particles.

Coals are classified according to rank. The rank increases in the order peat, lignite, sub-bituminous, bituminous, and anthracite. This increase in rank or coalification is accompanied by a decrease in volatile matter in the coal, an increase in the percentage of carbon (and thus, very importantly, a decrease in the percentage of hydrogen), and an increase in the percentage of oxygen.

On a microscopic level, coal is a mixture or aggregate of physically distinguishable and chemically different organic compounds, macerals, and inorganic minerals. Apparently the first attempt to classify coal was by Stopes,[9] who described four classes or lithotypes that on further examination proved to be macroscopic rather than microscopic. Thus, microscopic examination of the Stopes lithotypes revealed three fairly homogeneous petrographic constituents, now referred to as macerals, distinguished by the names, vitrinite, exinite (or liptinite), and inertinite:

- Inertinite: Unreactive or only slightly reactive in DCL.
- Exinite: Comparatively high hydrogen content, most aliphatic of the macerals, but tends to approach properties of vitrinite as coal rank increases.

The classification of coal is discussed in detail by Chiche,[10] who notes: "We are still using the International Classification of Coals, published in 1956, dividing coal into 10 classes, 3 groups and 5 subgroups."

With the knowledge that the inertinite was difficult to bring into solution in a DCL process, while the exinite had a higher hydrogen content and was more aliphatic, it made sense to evaluate the potential to manage the maceral content of coals to increase the DCL yield.[11] Such management is possible in that the macerals in a ground coal can be separated on the basis of density fractionation.

Practical techniques exist for separating coal macerals to produce relatively pure fractions of liptinite, vitrinite, and inertinite using a combination of multistage float and sink methods followed by density gradient centrifugation. As discussed above, indeed the susceptibility of the macerals to DCL was in the increasing order of inertinite, vitrinite, liptinite. However, the liquefaction efficiency of coals to date has not been consistent with maceral composition and thus petrographic investigations have not yet provided a model to predict liquefaction yield based on maceral makeup of a particular coal. Thus, additional work to understand the controlling mechanism remains to be done and little is yet known of the economics of either attempting to concentrate preferred macerals on a production basis (probably excessively expensive) or simply to identify certain coals as DCL susceptible, and then to mine and reserve them for this purpose.

Coal Chemical Composition and Chemistry

In spite of the significance of coal as a source of important chemicals and chemical knowledge, it has only been recently that the chemical structure of coal has been understood with some degree of confidence. This is not just the result of a lack of interest but the lack of necessary tools to interpret the structure. To unravel this structure has required over time the application of infrared spectroscopy, electron spin resonance, and most importantly H^+ and C^{2+} nuclear magnetic resonance.[12] Using available information, Wiser has generated a schematic

representation of the structural groups and connecting bridges in bituminous coal. The structural units are (benzene) ring structures varying
in the number of rings from one to as many as six or seven rings con-
densed together, with an average size unit of about three rings. The
conversion of the above structure to materials that would be gases or
liquids at room temperature requires breaking the connecting bridges to
produce free radicals, which in turn must be stabilized by adding hydrogen to the unsaturated bond of the free radical. There are various means
to rupture the connecting bridges and provide the hydrogen necessary
to saturate the bonds. These means will be reviewed briefly for the insight they provide to the methods of direct coal liquefaction.

The least severe conditions that will disrupt the bridges involves *solvent
extraction* to remove the soluble portion of the coal, using solvents such as
benzene, chloroform, or pyridine. This mild approach will extract materials such as straight chain parafins with carbon chains from C_{13} to C_{34}
and also some isoprenic compounds.

At temperatures of 100°C, acid-catalyzed depolymerization using an
alkylating agent such as phenol will cause disruption of $-CH_2-$ bridges
in the coal structure. Chiche shows that for certain coals the apparent
extraction yield can be as high as 75 percent, but this can be deceptive in
that some of the material is present as colloidal particles of high molecular weight.

Pyrolysis refers to the use of heat in the absence of air or another
reactive environment to rupture the bridge bonds at temperatures of
about 400–500°C. Hydrogen released from the coal at the same time can
combine with the ruptured bridge bonds to saturate the free radicals
produced in the rupturing process and thus stabilize the products. However, because the hydrogen content in the coal is insufficient to stabilize
all products at a molecular size that would correspond to liquids at room
temperature, many of the free radicals will combine with each other
through polymerization and condensation reactions to produce high-
molecular-weight solids. The atomic hydrogen content of a typical coal is
on the order 0.82 hydrogen atoms to 1.0 carbon atom, while typical
transportation fuels show H : C ratios of 2 : 1. Thus, only 41 percent of
the carbon in the typical coal could theoretically be converted to transportation products, with the remaining 59 percent of the carbon left
behind as a hydrogen depleted char.

The simple pyrolysis process can produce a higher yield of products by
providing a secondary source of hydrogen. Typically the secondary hydrogen source will be introduced in the form of a solvent, a "hydrogen
donor" solvent. The inorganic matter present in the coal may act as a
catalyst for adding the hydrogen to the free radicals produced by thermal disruption of the bridging bonds.

A variation of the above process involves the use of commercial catalysts to improve the yield of the reaction. A final permutation would be to eliminate the hydrogen donor solvent and catalytically hydrogenate the coal using high temperature gaseous hydrogen.

The Scientific Basis for DCL

The argument persists that there is an inadequate scientific basis to support DCL. The argument goes that with a better scientific basis the capability of the process to produce greater yields of more valuable products and, hence, achieve an economically competitive position with petroleum-derived fuels, would be achieved. But the process-oriented workers in the field argue that science lags behind the process developments rather than scientific developments leading to process innovations. Gorbaty[13,14] argues that a scientific understanding of coal's organic structure, inorganic structure, physical structure, and liquid characteristics would provide the basis for improving current conversion processes and establishing entirely new and more efficient and economic processes.

5 —————— HISTORY OF DIRECT COAL LIQUEFACTION DEVELOPMENT IN THE UNITED STATES

The early development of DCL up to 1944 was outlined in Chapter 4. Significant events in U.S. development of DCL are shown in Fig. 5.1, for the period 1944 to the present. As the time line shows, the first DCL plant operated in the United States at Louisiana, Missouri, used German technology, that is, catalytic hydrogenation with recycling of a process-derived solvent. This plant was operated until 1954 and was overlapped by a plant operated by Union Carbide at Institute, West Virginia, to provide chemical feedstocks in the period 1952 to 1956. This first U.S.-designed plant set the general trend of a departure from the German technology of 1927–1944, with its ever increasing hydrogen pressure and ever harsher process conditions. U.S. DCL developers were searching for conditions that would permit them to operate, in comparison with the German technology, at relatively lower temperature but more significantly at much lower hydrogen pressures. The lower pressure would permit the use of more typical oil refinery equipment and hopefully would reduce the rapid deterioration of pumps and pressure let-down valves experienced with the German technology.

In the following review of DCL technology, the approach used in Chapter 4 will again be followed. That is, we will proceed from the simplest technology to the most complex. In taking this approach in Chapter 4, we progressed from solvent extraction to two-stage catalytic hydrogenation. We are going to revise that approach here to reflect the fact that as the solvent extraction process has developed in the United States over the last thirty years, it has become more complex than the pyrolytic approach; in fact, the donor solvent processes are the fathers of

Figure 5.1.
Development of Direct Coal Liquefaction in the United States

		1944 The 78th Congress passed Public Law 290 Bureau of Mines to Study Large Scale Production of Synthetic Fuels From Coal and Other Substitutes
Semi-Commercial Plant, 50 Tons Per Day Using German Technology Operated at Louisana Missouri (Plant Closed in 1954)	1949	
		1952 Coal Hydrogenation Plant Developed by Union Carbide at Institute, West Virginia for Chemical Feedstock
Consol Synthetic Fuels Plant Developed by Consolidated Coal Company at Cresap, WV. 20 Ton Per Day Plant Operated to 1970 (Solvent Extraction-Catalytic Hydrogenation, Similar to Pott-Broche Process)	1963	
		1969 Development of the Synthoil Process Initiated by U.S. Bureau of Mines Pittsburgh Energy Research Center. Turbulent Flow of Coal-Oil Mixture Through Catalyst Bed
Arab Members of OPEC EmbargoShipments of Crude Oil to U. S.	1973	1973 Development of DOW Chemical of DCL Process Using Disposable Molybdenum Emulsion Catalyst
Chevron Research Company Begins Development of a Process Leading to Two Stage DCL	1974	
Operation of 6 Ton Per Day SRC-1 Plant Begins at Wilsonville, AL. Plant Modified in 1981 to Two Stage Process. Still in Operation	1974	1974 SRC 50 Ton Per Day Plant Becomes Fully Operational at Fort Lewis, WA. A Noncatalytic Solvent-Extraction-Hydrogenation Process, Still in Operation
		1975 Decision to Locate H Coal Plant Adjacent to Ashland Oil Inc. Refinery in Catlettsburg, KY. Process uses a Back Mixed Ebullanted Bed of Catalyst. The 200-600 Ton Per Day Plant Operated from 1980 to 1982.
		1979 Lummus Integrated Two Stage Liquefaction Under Development by Lummus-Crest. Two Stage Process Permits Optimazation of Coal Dissolution and Hydrogen Process.

Figure 5.1. (Continued)

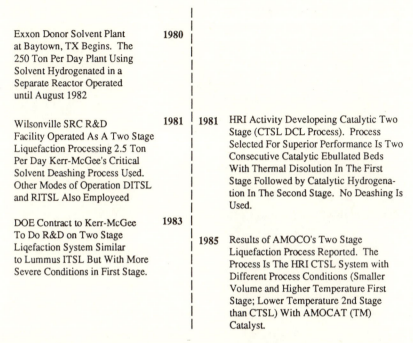

Exxon Donor Solvent Plant at Baytown, TX Begins. The 250 Ton Per Day Plant Using Solvent Hydrogenated in a Separate Reactor Operated until August 1982	1980		
Wilsonville SRC R&D Facility Operated As A Two Stage Liquefaction Processing 2.5 Ton Per Day Kerr-McGee's Critical Solvent Deashing Process Used. Other Modes of Operation DITSL and RITSL Also Employeed	1981	1981	HRI Activity Developeing Catalytic Two Stage (CTSL DCL Process). Process Selected For Superior Performance Is Two Consecutive Catalytic Ebullated Beds With Thermal Disolution In The First Stage Followed by Catalytic Hydrogenation In The Second Stage. No Deashing Is Used.
DOE Contract to Kerr-McGee To Do R&D on Two Stage Liqefaction System Similar to Lummus ITSL But With More Severe Conditions in First Stage.	1983	1985	Results of AMOCO's Two Stage Liquefaction Process Reported. The Process Is The HRI CTSL System with Different Process Conditions (Smaller Volume and Higher Temperature First Stage; Lower Temperature 2nd Stage than CTSL) With AMOCAT (TM) Catalyst.

Sources: Based in part on information provided by David Gray, Energy Resources and Environmental Division, MITRE Corp., Washington Center, McLean, VA; P. Nowacki, *Coal Liquefaction Processes,* Noyes Data Corp., Park Ridge, NJ (1977); W. R. K. Wu, and H. H. Storch, "Hydrogenation of Coal and Tar," Bureau of Mines Bulletin 63 (1968); E. L. Sawy, A. Gray, A. Talib, and G. Tomlinson, "A Techno-Economic Assessment of Recent Advancements in Direct Coal Liquefaction," MITRE Metrek Division, McLean, VA, SAND 86-7103 (June 1986).

the two-stage catalytic technique. Thus, this review will begin with the various applications of pyrolysis.

PYROLYSIS

This process has been historically known as carbonization, destructive distillation, and also as retorting. It is an old process that has been used to produce coke, coal gas, coal tar, and chemicals since 1850. Coal heated in the absence of air, or specifically oxygen, yields gases, light liquids, heavy liquids, and finally a solid char. The simple retorting process can be made more complex to increase the yield of desired products by adding hydrogen and/or recirculating vapors derived from the process. Other process variables include:

- heating rate;
- maximum temperature;
- coal and product residence time;
- coal particle size;
- retort configuration.

Experience has shown that yield increases with decreasing particle size and residence time and increasing heat rate. Advantages of the process include:

- pressures may be low;
- hydrogen addition is not required;
- the equipment is simple.

But the disadvantages are also significant:

- only half of the coal charged is converted to liquids;
- the remaining char or coke is high in sulfur and has no significant market or market value;
- a significant amount of the heavy oil cannot be readily separated from the entrained solids;
- the liquid products are not ready for use as fuels and require removal of heteroatoms and upgrading through hydrogenation to a useful commercial-quality level.

The last point, hydrogenation of products, raises the concept of integrating hydrogenation into the pyrolytic process. This approach will be reviewed at the end of this discussion.

In-depth reviews of the pyrolysis approach are provided by Goldman,[1] Nowaki,[2] and Wiser,[3,4,5] with extensive coverage of the patent literature on the subject. Limiting the discussion to modern improvements of this ancient process, the above authors particularly singled out the char-to-energy development (COED) process as one of the most successful pyrolysis approaches. In this process, liquids were recovered from a mixture with char solids using filter aids and precoated rotary filters. This process worked remarkably well considering the fineness of the char solids and the viscous nature of the liquids. This oil showed an H : C atom ratio of about 1.1 : 1, or roughly half of what would be required for a typical transportation fuel. Thus hydrogenation of the oil COED product would be required. The oil also contained the hetro atoms O, N, and S, in atom to hydrogen ratios of 0.46 : 1, 0.07 : 1, and 0.006 : 1, respectively; these would also be expected to be significantly reduced in the hydrogenation process. At the end of this process, however, only a syn-crude would be produced, which would require further refining before the product would be commercially useful. Because of the low yield of the process, the lack of a market for the char, and the low value of the product oil, interest in the COED process terminated about 1977.

A fundamentally different pyrolysis approach has been developed by Occidental Research Corporation (ORC). It was known that the yield of coal liquefaction improved with decreasing particle size and residence time and increasing heat. The object of the ORC process design was to heat the coal to decomposition temperature in as short a time as possible and then to remove the decomposition vapor and quench the temperature as rapidly as possible to prevent repolymerization.

The ORC flash pyrolysis process[6,7] was designed to take advantage of the above characteristics. The ORC process, after finely dividing the coal, combined it with hot recycled char to raise the coal to 950 to 1350°F. To produce rapid coal heating it was necessary to use a char recirculation rate of 5–10 times the coal charging rate. The vapor volatilized from the coal is separated from the char in the cyclone separator. The char is partially recovered as product while the remainder is partially burned to raise the temperature to 1200–1700°F to heat the incoming coal feed. The recovered vapor is collected in a water quench system after which the product liquid is split into a light oil, which is recycled, and a product tar. The tar, of course, would have to be hydrogenated to produce liquid fuels.

In tests performed in a semicontinuous reactor, what were considered excellent results were obtained. These tests showed a maximum conversion of 35 percent of the coal to liquids; that was significantly better than what was achieved with the COED process. However, results obtained with a PDU in April 1977 showed a yield of only 10 percent liquid. Through various improvements in equipment and process the yield was increased to 30 percent after mid-1978. However, the ORC process was plagued with continuing problems that included:

- reactor fouling;
- poor char distribution and circulation rate fluctuations;
- poor mechanical reliability; weld and valve failures.

Operation of the PDU was suspended by June 1979.

There have been a number of other attempts to develop pyrolysis-based processes that would take advantage of the simplicity of this process and at the same time produce liquid yields that would satisfy the still substantial costs. Representative processes include the clean coke process,[8] TOSCO,[9] "Coalcon,"[10] Oak Ridge hydrocarbonization process,[11]

Brookhaven National Laboratory flash hydropyrolysis lignite process,[12] Rocketdyne flash hydrogenation process,[13] and the Lurgi flash carbonization process.[14,15] All of these processes suffer from the fact that the liquid yields are low and generally require further hydrogenation of the liquid to produce commercially useful product. The solid product does not have a market that will justify the cost of producing it.

SOLVENT EXTRACTION: SOLVENT REFINED COAL

As discussed in Chapter 4, the solvent extraction process can range from the simple solution of those portions of the coal that can be extracted with particular solvents to the high temperature donor solvent processes that are the forerunners of today's second generation two-stage liquefaction processes. The basic approach in a modern solvent extraction process is not simply to put the soluble portion of the coal into solution but, by the use of high temperatures (up to 950°F) and the application of high pressure, to put a high fraction of the organic portion of the coal into solution, break the CH_2 bond bridges in the molecule, and then saturate the free radicals produced, thus stabilizing them and ending with a high yield of liquid products. The general advantages of the solvent extraction approach are:

• less severe operating temperature than encountered in pyrolysis;
• can be adapted to meet the characteristics of different coal feeds.

The disadvantages include:

• a hydrogen source is required, with its accompanying economic penalty;
• higher pressures required than in the pyrolysis process, and hence more exotic equipment;
• it is very difficult to separate entrained solids from the liquid product;
• the liquid product generally requires further hydrogenation to be commercially useful;
• the solid product has little commercial interest or value.

The solvent extraction DCL processes are exhaustively reviewed in two publications by the Noyes Data Corporation and there is little point in reviewing that detail here.[16,17] However, several of the processes falling into this category are sufficiently different from each other, and also because they serve as a means of describing progress in the development of the second-generation, two-stage catalytic conversion processes, that they deserve a brief review. These include the SRC II and EDS processes, also reviewed by Wiser.[18]

The SRC II process produces low sulfur synthetic fuel oil and a lower boiling naphtha product. The process is a variation of the Pott-Broche process developed in Germany and patented there in 1932. SRC is distinguished by the fact that it has gone through a period of transition from SRC I to SRC II and back to SRC I. The differences in the plant can to some degree be described in terms of the differences in the products. SRC I was designed to produce a solid coal-like boiler fuel with less than 1 percent sulfur and 0.2 percent ash. The process and its evolution have been of particular interest to the utility industry, with support of the SRC I plant at Wilsonville, Alabama, by the Southern Company Services and the Edison Electric Institute (EEI) with the Electric Power Research Institute (EPRI) taking over EEI's responsibilities in 1973. A second SCR plant was built at Ft. Lewis, Washington and operated there by Pittsburgh and Midway Coal Company (a subsidiary of Gulf Oil Corp.) with a laboratory unit at Merriam, Kansas, serving both SRC I and SRC II with tests simulating and evaluating process variables for the two pilot plants.

SRC I converted high sulfur and ash coals to a low sulfur solid fuel by mixing pulverized coal with a process-derived solvent and heating the slurry in the presence of 1500 psi hydrogen gas to 800–875°F in an upward flow reactor. In the residence time of thirty minutes, 93 percent of the coal is dissolved to form hydrocarbons from methane to light oil while converting the sulfur in the coal to H_2S. In a separator the gases are stripped off while the liquids and undissolved solids are separated by filtration. The solids, including unreacted coal, are gasified to produce makeup hydrogen using the shift reaction while the liquids are separated in the solvent recovery unit to produce recycled solvent as a light liquid and the solid solvent is refined to produce low sulfur/ash coal. The gas stream is treated to recover elemental sulfur and hydrogen for recycling. The SRC coal product has a solidification point of about 350°F and a heating value of about 16,000 Btu/lb.

The SRC II process differed from SRC I in that after the dissolver a portion of the dissolved product was recycled to blend with the incoming coal for return to the dissolver, which was operated at an increased reactor pressure and residence time compared with SRC I. The product in this case could be fractionated to produce naphtha, low sulfur oil, and a vacuum residue of heavy oil, ash, and unreacted organic coal matter. The yield of liquids from the SRC II process ranged from about 30 to 40 percent by weight of the moisture-free coal feed.

The SRC pilot plants have also acted as test beds for some important developments that have more general interest:

• Addition of iron pyrite to increase liquid yield.
• The development of critical solvent de-ashing.[19]

- Refinement of practice of routinely using centrifugal separators to remove solids from liquid product.

Development of the Exxon Donor Solvent Process (EDS)[20,21] was characterized by a seven year pre-analysis to define a flow sheet that had the potential to produce commercial products as close to a competitive price as possible. An attempt was made to use equipment that was as similar as possible to that used in refinery practice. Based on these considerations, a hydrogenated recycle solvent process using a noncatalytic open tubular plug flow reactor with vacuum separation of products was selected for evaluation.

The advantages of this approach were expected to be:

- The coal solids did not come into contact with catalyst, thus extending catalyst lifetime.
- The plant minimized the use of both process fuel and hydrogen.
- Use of refining equipment would enhance the possibility of refinery adoption while reducing equipment costs.
- The hydrogenated solvent process produced liquids that were readily separated from the solids.

In pilot studies, EDS produced high yields of low sulfur liquids from bituminous and sub-bituminous coals and lignites. However, liquid yields on a moisture-free basis averaged 33 percent and thus there remained an economic need to improve the yield of commercially valued liquid products.

CATALYTIC HYDROGENATION

This was the process developed by Germany prior to WWII and used during the war to provide the bulk of Nazi Germany's aviation fuel. The United States evaluated the German process at Louisiana, Missouri, up to 1954. In the DCL studies that followed in the 1960s, the objective was to reduce process severity and exposure compared with German practice, thus reducing the need for equipment to withstand very high temperature, high pressure hydrogen environments.

Certainly one of the more significant developments in the history of DCL in the United States is the H-Coal process.[22,23] H-Coal is an adaptation of the H-Oil process, a catalytic process to convert heavy oil petroleum residues into lighter commercially valuable liquids. The H-Oil and H-Coal processes make use of an ebullated (highly back-mixed) bed of catalyst in a fluidized state. The process begins with pulverized dry coal (minus 60 mesh) being slurried with a recycled process-derived solvent and pumped with hydrogen at a pressure of 200 atm (the WWII

Table 5.1.
Lummus Clean Fuels from Coal Process (LCFFC)

Invented in 1972 to overcome the technical and economic limitations of single-stage coal liquefaction processes (e.g., H-coal).

Incorporates two or more expanded-bed hydrocrackers in series without the need for external recycle to second and third reactors.

Avantages include:

- Nearly plug-flow design
- No internal recycle: Ebullation maintained by fresh feed kinetic energy
- Temperature gradient exists along the coal liquefaction reaction path
- Minimizes gas formation and hydrogen consumption
- Reduced backmixing

Tested in a one-half TPD PDU operated during 1977–1979

The interest in CFFC lies in the following points:

- Use of multistage plug flow ebullated reactors to minimize hydrogen consumption.
- Evaluation of cobalt molybdate, tungsten nickel sulfide, nickel molybdate, or mixtures of these catalysts.
- Incorporation of a critical solvent de-ashing process in the flow sheet.

German processes used minimum pressures of 290 atm) to the reactor at a temperature of 650–750°F, to maintain the 850°F operating temperature in the ebullated bed. Although hydrogen recovery is employed, there is a need for makeup hydrogen. Thus, as with H-Oil, the H-Coal plant would need to be located in proximity to a hydrogen source (e.g., a petroleum refinery). The design yield was 47 percent of C_4 to 950°F boiling oils.

Another catalytic hydrogenation process of interest is the clean fuels from coal (CFFC) process developed by Lummus Crest. The objectives and status of the process are described in Table 5.1.[24]

TWO-STAGE INTEGRATED LIQUEFACTION

The present status of DCL is defined in terms of the integrated two-stage liquefaction processes. As noted in Chapter 4, the Germans recognized the potential of integrated two stage liquefaction in 1943. The concept is simply that DCL involves two distinct processes: (1) the solution of the coal in a solvent; and (2) the catalytic hydrogenation of the solubilized coal to produce products of the desired specification. Different processes will use different operating conditions. For example, most of the two stage processes will use a higher first stage temperature than second stage temperature while the HRI catalytic two-stage process (CTSL) reverses this practice. Some processes will use catalyst in both stages while others will use solvent de-ashing. The proponents of processes that don't use de-ashing claim that by closely integrating the two stages and not using de-ashing, they are reducing heat loss from the process. They also note that through good control of product specification in the second stage, they have no significant problem in separating products and solids and recirculation of solids with recycled liquid to the first stage does not detract but enhances process yield and product specification.

A recent publication compares and contrasts the six leading integrated two-stage liquefaction processes[25] and then compares them in terms of process and economics with the H-Coal and EDS catalytic hydrogenation processes. Rather than reproducing that information here, the reader is referred to the work of El Sawy, et al.

After reviewing the information in the available literature, the question of what is the objective of DCL development can be asked. There are two points typically made in reply:

- produce commercially valuable liquid products from coal; and
- produce those products at a competitive price.

Process results indicate that the first point has been achieved. We have a number of processes developed to the level experts describe as "commercial." These processes, in the opinion of some engineers, are capable of being scaled to commercial size and will produce products at a price we can estimate. Tables 5.2 and 5.3 (from El Sawy, et al.) provide prices in dollars (1981) per barrel for several two-stage integrated processes and for comparison purposes prices for two single-stage processes, H-Coal and EDS. Results are presented for an Illinois No. 6 coal and a Wyoming sub-bituminous coal in, respectively, Tables 5.2 and 5.3.

In agreement with the results in Tables 5.2 and 5.3, experts, when asked what price oil would be required to make the products of DCL competitive, state the price to be between $40 to $50 per bbl of crude. Experience of the last fourteen years has shown, however, that if the price of oil went that high, inflation would certainly significantly increase the capital cost of DCL plants. The data presented are based on capital costs that vary from 36 to 46 percent of total production cost; thus these prices are very sensitive to capital cost. Therefore, it is unlikely that at a world crude oil price of $40–50 per bbl, the integrated two-stage processes would still be competitive; the product prices presented in these two tables would be expected to increase significantly.

Therefore, with regard to the second point above, the most advanced

Table 5.2.

PLANT ECONOMICS SUMMARY - COSTS IN MILLION 1981 DOLLARS

ILLINOIS No. 6 COAL PLANTS

	LUMMAS ITSL	WILSONVILLE ITSL	WILSONVILLE DITSL	MODIFIED LIMMUS ITSL	AMOCO	CTSL	H-COAL	EDS
Plant Construction Cost	2,509	2,535	2,566	2,554	2,556	2,592	2,360	2,249
Total Capital Required	4,032	4,084	4,142	4,112	4,118	4,184	3,315	3,648
Annual Capital Recovery Cost	552	560	567	563	564	573	523	500
Coal Cost	356	384	407	382	389	414	367	362
Other Operating Cost	347	350	352	351	351	354	337	330
ByProduct Credit	43	43	43	43	43	43	43	43
Hydrotreating Cost	233	253	194	236	252	255	297	146
Raw Product Price Analysis								
Eq. MB/SD Raw Product	90.1	97.0	101.5	95.3	93.8	107.4	92.1	85.2
Annual Revenue Requirement	1,212	1,251	1,283	1,253	1,261	1,298	1,184	1,293
Required Selling Price, $/B	40.80	39.05	38.53	39.78	40.75	36.63	38.95	46.05
Hydrotreated Product Price Analysis								
Eq. MB/SD Hydrotreated Product	100.7	106.1	109.7	107.3	100.2	116.5	99.3	85.2
Annual Revenue Requirement	1,445	1,504	1,477	1,489	1,513	1,553	1,481	1,295
Required Selling Price, $/B	43.49	42.94	40.84	42.06	45.76	40.41	45.20	46.05

Table 5.3.
PLANT ECONOMICS SUMMARY - COSTS IN MILLION 1981 DOLLARS

WYOMING COAL PLANTS

	LUMMAS ITSL	WILSONVILLE ITSL	WILSONVILLE DITSL	CTSL	H-COAL	EDS
Plant Construction Cost	2,599	2,668	2,523	2,634	2,429	2,287
Total Capital Required	4,062	4,173	3,957	4,131	3,814	3,597
Annual Capital Recovery Cost	557	572	542	566	522	493
Coal Cost	124	135	136	159	133	125
Other Operating Cost	353	362	352	357	342	332
ByProduct Credit	16	16	16	16	16	16
Hydrotreating Cost	246	183	172	165	144	119
Raw Product Price Analysis						
Eq. MB/SD Raw Product	72.8	89.5	95.6	112.7	89.3	76.7
Annual Revenue Requirement	1,018	1,053	1,014	1,066	991	934
Required Selling Price, $/B	42.41	35.67	32.16	28.69	33.33	36.91
Hydrotreated Product Price Analysis						
Eq. MB/SD Hydrotreated Product	83.1	93.3	96.7	117.6	92.1	76.1
Annual Revenue Requirement	1,264	1,236	1,186	1,231	1,125	1,053
Required Selling Price, $/B	46.10	40.15	37.20	31.75	37.03	41.93

DCL processes do not produce products at a competitive price and the panel of experts agree they do not see the potential for incremental improvements in present processes or similar processes changing that conclusion. A radically new and different process would be required; something that would decrease cost about a factor of two.

6 ——————————— H-COAL: THE BASELINE CASE

INTRODUCTION

A baseline case has been developed for this study as a means of bench-marking many of the technical, economic, and policy factors associated with the development of direct coal liquefaction processes. H-Coal is a typical DCL process in that it is a "proven" technology; a great deal of money, both public and private, has been invested in the technology; and the process has not been commercialized in the United States. Many other existing DCL technologies fit this description (SRC, Lummus, and EDS) and many of the newer two-stage DCL technologies can be characterized by at least one of these factors.

H-Coal uses an ebullated-bed reactor to convert coal to liquid products. It is a direct catalytic hydro-liquefaction process that evolved from the H-oil process of Hydrocarbon Research, Inc. In the process, coal is pulverized, slurried with process-derived oil, and pumped into the bottom of the reactor. The coal slurry, which partially dissolves as it passes through a preheater, is combined with hydrogen and a catalyst (aluminum oxide-based extrudates impregnated with the sulfides of cobalt or nickel and molybdenum) in the ebullating bed reactor. The advantage of the ebullating bed design is that portions of the catalyst are removed and refreshed without interruption to the process. The reactor products are depressurized and fractionated after leaving the reactor vessel. A variety of petroleum products are produced depending upon the severity of the process.

This chapter will begin with a short history of H-coal. A time line is

Figure 6.1.
H-Coal Timeline

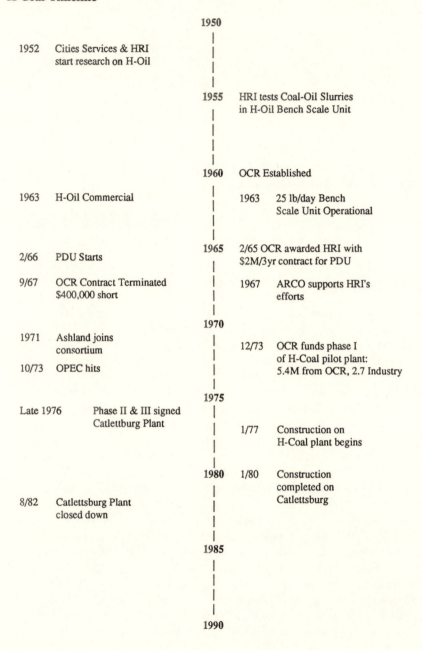

1950

1952   Cities Services & HRI
         start research on H-Oil

1955   HRI tests Coal-Oil Slurries
         in H-Oil Bench Scale Unit

1960   OCR Established

1963   H-Oil Commercial

           1963   25 lb/day Bench
                   Scale Unit Operational

1965   2/65 OCR awarded HRI with
2/66   PDU Starts $2M/3yr contract for PDU

9/67   OCR Contract Terminated
         $400,000 short   1967   ARCO supports HRI's
                                efforts

1970

1971   Ashland joins
         consortium   12/73   OCR funds phase I
10/73   OPEC hits   of H-Coal pilot plant:
                                5.4M from OCR, 2.7 Industry

1975

Late 1976   Phase II & III signed
                     Catlettburg Plant

                            1/77   Construction on
                                H-Coal plant begins

1980   1/80   Construction
                                completed on
8/82   Catlettsburg Plant   Catlettsburg
         closed down

1985

1990

shown in Fig. 6.1. It will be followed by three sections providing policy, technological, and economic explanations for the development of H-coal. Throughout the remainder of this report, the H-coal baseline case will be revisited as a means of illustrating various points and as an RTA tool for validating the conclusions.

A SHORT HISTORY OF H-COAL

In 1952, the petroleum industry was on the upswing. Cities Services and Development Corporation and Hydrocarbon Research, Inc. (HRI) initiated a research program to develop a process to upgrade residual oil through hydrogenation. Residual oil is a high boiling, low grade petroleum product produced through the distillation of crude oil. Residual fuel sells at a much lower price than gasoline or heating fuel. Cities Services and HRI found that gasoline, aviation fuel, and middle distillate fuels can be produced when residual oil reacts with hydrogen in the presence of a catalyst. In addition, the process, H-oil, reduces the sulfur and ash content of the oil and produces char that can be converted into hydrogen for reuse in the process.[1]

In 1955, HRI began testing coal-oil slurries in an H-oil bench-scale unit. HRI researchers undoubtedly were familiar with Germany's efforts to hydrogenate coal during World War II. Knowledge gained through further H-oil research indicated that HRI had made substantial improvements to the German process. Specifically, the H-oil process afforded much lower operating pressures, better temperature control, and more efficient conversion of the coal to synthetic oil.[2] In 1961, HRI patented the concept and named it H-Coal.

While research continued on H-coal, H-oil rapidly advanced to the commercial stage. Cities Services hired HRI to design and construct the first commercial installation of an oil hydrogenation plant at their refinery in Lake Charles, Louisiana. The plant went into operation in 1963 and processed 2500 barrels per day of low-grade crude and residual oils. Contracts were signed shortly thereafter with HRI to construct H-oil plants in New Jersey and Kuwait.

The next step in developing H-coal was the construction of a bench-scale unit. The HRI unit was designed to test 25 pounds of coal per day. It quickly became clear to HRI in the early 1960s that this new method could efficiently manufacture low-sulfur liquid fuels from coal.

During the mid-1960s, a process development unit was constructed with funding by the Office of Coal Research (OCR). The process demonstration unit (PDU) could process 2.5 tons of coal per day and had a reactor diameter of 8.5 inches. HRI's objective with the PDU was to demonstrate a continuous H-coal operation while checking this performance against bench-scale tests. Researchers at HRI were especially concerned with controlling catalytic reaction in the reactor and maximizing output through altering the balance among the various inputs. Bench-scale operations continued to provide useful information on the effect of operating parameters and catalyst age on the conversion of a variety of coals.

Operation of the PDU started in February 1966. By 1969, the bench-scale unit had achieved slightly over 8000 hours of operation, with 6000 of those hours testing Illinois No. 6 coal. A continuous run of 473 hours (Run #5) was achieved with the PDU utilizing Illinois coal. It was during this run that the catalyst withdrawal system was demonstrated, which is a critical feature of the ebullating bed technology.

A consortium of private sponsors became involved in the H-coal project after federal funding was terminated in 1967. However, in late 1973, at the genesis of the energy crisis, the federal government agreed to fund (in conjunction with a private sector consortium) the first phase of an H-coal pilot plant. The plant, which was sited in Catlettsburg, Kentucky, was constructed between January 1977 and December 1979 under a joint funding arrangement between the U.S. Department of Energy, the Kentucky Department of Energy (KDOE), HRI, Ashland Oil Company, and a consortium of private sector sponsors. The plant was designed to process 200–600 tons of coal per day.

Operation of the plant began in March 1980 and terminated in August 1982. One of the most successful runs was with Illinois bituminous coal from August 7 to December 11, 1981 (Run #8). Over the 131 day period, 19,200 tons of pulverized dried coal were converted into approximately 57,600 barrels of naphtha and distillate oils.

Ashland Oil Company proposed to build a commercial scale plant in Breckinridge, Kentucky. However, the plant never proceeded beyond the design phase due to a variety of concerns.

POLICY ISSUES

From a policy perspective, there were four important decisions regarding H-coal that significantly influenced its development. These decisions were: (1) a February 1965 OCR award of $2 million to HRI to build and operate a PDU; (2) a September 1967 decision by OCR to prematurely terminate HRI's contract; (3) a December 1973 decision by OCR to fund Phase I of an H-coal pilot plant; and (4) a late 1976 award of $143.2 million by the Energy Research and Development Administration (OCR's successor agency) to construct and operate an H-Coal pilot plant. Each one of these events will be discussed in detail below. Here the focus will be on the policy arena in which these decisions were made and the importance of the policy environment in shaping the development of a direct coal liquefaction technology.

OCR's Decision to Fund a Process Development Unit

Until the early 1960s, funding for research on H-coal came from the private sector. The developer of the process, HRI, was also the primary supporter. HRI was able to devote resources to H-coal through funds provided by Cities Services, Inc. to develop the H-oil process.

During the early 1960s, pertinent DCL policy decisions were made in Washington, D.C. Throughout the Eisenhower administration, the interests of the coal industry were subsidiary to nuclear and petroleum concerns. After repeated attempts in Congress, President Eisenhower finally signed into law on July 7, 1960, a bill establishing the Office of Coal Research (OCR) under the Department of the Interior.[3] This boost in coal research and development gained support from Eisenhower for two reasons. First, additional government support and incentives in the natural gas and petroleum industries seemingly placed the coal industry at a disadvantage. Second, the Eisenhower administration viewed the coal industry more as a problem of unemployment than as an energy development alternative.[4] OCR addressed both of these concerns by promoting the development of alternative uses of coal that ultimately could revive this declining industry and its associated production regions.

One of the major beneficiaries of OCR's funding was HRI. In February 1965 OCR awarded HRI a $2 million, 3 year contract to continue its research on the H-coal process. This grant came at a critical point in the H-coal research and development effort. Preliminary results from the 25 pound per day bench-scale unit indicated that the hydrogenation method was technically feasible and potentially economically competitive with conventional fuels. However, the bench-scale unit was much too small (reactor diameter was 0.75 inches) and far too simple to gain a complete understanding of the conversion process. HRI's next step was to build a process development unit (PDU) with a coal feed rate of 2.5 tons per day. OCR funding was directed at the construction of this unit with continued research at the bench-scale level.

OCR's Termination of PDU Funds

Suddenly, in September 1967, the OCR contract with HRI was terminated, approximately $400,000 short of the original funding level. George M. Fumich, then head of the OCR, explained in a 1968 appropriations hearing,

We had a choice. We knew we weren't going to get enough money to carry the project on into a pilot plant where it should go as a next phase. On the other hand, if we continued to carry it on at the then existing level, we would be wasting government money.[5]

Ironically, at the same hearings just one year earlier, Fumich told Congress that OCR "anticipated heading into the pilot-plant phase [with H-coal]. The process has reached a point where a pilot can be built."[6] Supporting long-term, capital-intensive coal conversion research, which was OCR's mandate, soon became difficult to maintain. Though OCR's budget continued to grow in the 1960s, the Office found it difficult to commit funds to multi-year programs while also initiating new ones. This problem was compounded when projects exceeded their budgets and OCR was forced to fund the cost overruns. For example, Project Gasoline, which was designed and operated by Consolidation Coal Company and funded by OCR, was expected to cost $9 million to complete in 1965. By 1969, that figure had jumped to $20 million. OCR, faced with a choice of continuing Project Gasoline, which was near commercialization, or funding several less-developed technologies, opted to continue Project Gasoline. It is interesting to note that, for technical reasons, Project Gasoline never became operational at the commercial scale.

However, the loss of OCR funding, while initially debilitating, actually assisted in the development of the technology. Without government support, HRI was forced to search for corporate sponsors. Atlantic Richfield Corporation (ARCO) immediately began to sponsor HRI's research in 1967. This corporate sponsorship played an important role in later attempts to fund a pilot project.

Oil company sponsorship of synthetic fuel technologies was not unusual during this period. ARCO, like several other petroleum companies, did not want to lose a share of the synfuels market if and when these coal conversion technologies were commercialized. Investment in these technologies usually yielded a share of the domestic licensing royalties or granted the company rights to the patent. In addition to supporting the technologies, these companies were purchasing large coal fields. Ashland Oil, for example, founded Arch Minerals Corporation in 1969, which was producing over 3 million tons of coal by 1971.[7]

ARCO was not a newcomer to the synthetic fuels industry. It conducted an in-house research program, which patented several new coal conversion techniques in the early 1970s.[8] HRI, with ARCO support, tested a wide range of coals from 1967 to 1969. Several HRI researchers reported in 1969 that they had presented a proposal to OCR to construct and operate a 250 ton per day (tpd) demonstration plant.[9] Though OCR agreed in principle with the proposal, their funding levels precluded their support of the demonstration plant.

Sponsorship of the H-coal research further broadened in the early 1970s to include several additional industrial concerns. Ashland Oil, Exxon, Gulf, Consolidated Coal, Sunoco, and Standard of Indiana provided support through "purchase of technology agreements." These agreements grant H-coal patent rights to these firms, allowing them to commercialize the process without any royalty payments.

Ashland, which provided $250,000, was the largest contributor to the consortium. Like ARCO, Ashland had some experience with synthetic fuels. Ashland started to research coal conversion techniques in the early to mid-1960s when they realized that oil resources were not limitless. For six years, they operated a small in-house research program. In 1971, Ashland concluded that it was worthwhile to conduct additional research on Eastern coal conversion, using a direct rather than indirect liquefaction technique.[10] Ashland's goal as a member of the consortium was to test a variety of coals, including Kentucky coal, in HRI's units and PDU.

Phase I Funding of the H-Coal Pilot Plant

October 16, 1973, is a date that will be well remembered in history. War raged in the Middle East and the Organization of Petroleum Exporting Countries (OPEC) cut off supplies of oil to the United States in a protest against U.S. pro-Israeli foreign policy. For the first time in the history of the nation, a national energy policy and the bureaucracy to implement it was developed, by the Nixon administration. An integral component of this plan, later known as Project Independence, was a massive research and development effort in synthetic fuels. Once again, the federal government was interested in the H-coal process.

The growth in coal research funding during this period was spectacular. The OCR budget of $43 million in 1973 grew to $261 million two years later. H-Coal was an early beneficiary of this expanded research effort. In December 1973, OCR agreed to fund Phase I of a H-coal pilot plant. Like many large projects, the pilot plant proposal was divided into three phases: design, construction, and operation. Phase I, which was estimated to cost $8.1 million, continued PDU testing, designed the pilot plant, and conducted an environmental assessment of the process. OCR provided $5.4 million while a consortium of industrial firms, composed of Ashland Oil, ARCO, Standard of Indiana, Shell, Sunoco, and the Electric Power Research Institute, contributed $2.7 million.

Three locations were originally proposed for the siting of the H-coal pilot plant. Sun Oil (Sunoco) offered a site near Tulsa, Oklahoma; Exxon proposed a site in southern Illinois; and Ashland Oil offered a site in Catlettsburg, Kentucky. A comprehensive study of the sites was conducted for HRI, based on the total estimated cost of the program if it were to be placed at one of these locations.

Ashland was very interested in locating the H-coal facility in Catlettsburg. However, given the fact that most of the H-coal research had been conducted with Illinois and Wyodak (Wyoming) coal, it seemed both practical and economical to locate the plant near these seams. Ashland was certainly at a geographic disadvantage. However, Ashland had an overwhelming advantage over the other sites in the form of a major supporter—the Commonwealth of Kentucky.

Kentucky, a coal-rich state, has been a strong backer of proposals that seek to utilize their vast energy resource. As a Kentucky Department of Energy official noted, Ashland presented the Commonwealth with an "opportunity" when it came to the state with the H-coal proposal in 1974.[11] Ashland easily convinced Kentucky of the technical virtues of H-coal. It was also clear that the Commonwealth would stand to benefit if the process used Kentucky coal and the plant employed Kentucky residents. Wendall Ford, governor of Kentucky at the time, was also a strong supporter of the Catlettsburg site. In an effort to guarantee the placement of the plant in Kentucky, Ford made three commitments to the project. First, Kentucky would donate 88,000 tons of coal to the project. Second, the Commonwealth would establish a $2.5 million coal equalization fund to cover the cost of non-Kentucky coal transported to the site. Third, the Commonwealth would donate $3.9 million from their Energy Development and Demonstration Trust Fund to the project. In addition, some research support would be provided by the University of Kentucky's Institute for Mining and Minerals Research. The total support package amounted to approximately $8 million.

As a result of the incentives from the Commonwealth and with an agreement from Ashland to provide certain services and materials to the pilot plant, HRI recommended to OCR that the H-coal plant be placed in Catlettsburg.[12] Eventually, the site was approved by the federal government.

After some initial disagreement as to the exact location of the plant in Catlettsburg, a site adjacent to the Ashland Petroleum Company refinery was chosen. This forty-three acre plot of land, which is directly south of the town of Catlettsburg (population 4000), is bordered by the Big Sandy River to the East.

Phases II and III, Award to Construct and Operate the Pilot Plant

A major reorganization in the federal government resulted in the creation of the Energy Research and Development Agency (ERDA) in October 1974. The functions of OCR and many other energy-oriented divisions in various parts of the federal government were centralized through the establishment of ERDA. As Phase I design plans were being developed by HRI, ERDA was evaluating Phase II and Phase III of the H-coal Project. In late 1976 a standard contractual agreement was signed between ERDA and a consortium of seven private sponsors for Phases II and III. The private sponsors (Ashland, HRI, KDOE, EPRI, Mobil, Standard Oil of Indiana, and Conoco Coal Development Company) agreed to fund 20 percent, or $35.6 million, while the federal government contributed 80 percent, or $143.2 million. The contract also protected the private sponsors from sharing in possible cost overruns through a cost-sharing ceiling. This ceiling limited their contributions to $38 million.

The pilot plant was designed to process between 200 to 600 tons of coal per day. This represents a scale-up factor of 100 from the PDU. Construction of the plant was slated to be completed in September 1978. The plant would operate for two years (January 1980–December 1981) and then would be dismantled. Ashland Oil's subsidiary, Ashland Synthetic Fuels Inc. (ASFI), was placed in charge of both constructing and operating the plant.

At this point, it is interesting to highlight the terminology that was used to ensure the largest amount of government funding for the pilot plant. It was clear from the beginning of the design stage that the next step after the pilot plant would be a commercial-size plant. A 1978 report by ASFI stated, "the prime function of the H-Coal plant program is to provide data for the design and construction of a commercial coal liquefaction plant based on the H-Coal process."[13] The jump from the pilot plant to the commercial plant omits the demonstration stage, which is traditionally included in pioneering process plant research and development. A demonstration plant differs from a pilot plant in that it is a full-scale prototype of an operational plant. Additionally, a pilot plant is characterized by semi-continuous operation with runs lasting from days to several weeks while the demonstration plant is designed to operate continuously.[14]

With the division between a pilot plant and a demonstration plant being somewhat nebulous, the Catlettsburg plant could have been labeled with either title. Charles Hoertz, an ASFI official, simply argued that a demonstration plant was not necessary: "We don't see, after building this pilot plant out here, that we need a demonstration plant."[15] At the time that the decision was made to construct the plant, the terminology of the plant was as much a political move as it was technical. In 1976, it was the policy of ERDA to fund only 50 percent of a demonstration project while a pilot plant could receive up to 80 percent of federal funding. Ashland and the consortium of private sponsors were able to minimize their contributions and ultimately their share of the risk of the project by calling the Catlettsburg plant a pilot facility.

Policy decisions have played an important role in the development of H-coal. The federal government funded the technology at two critical stages in the technology development process: the construction and operation of first the PDU and then the pilot plant. Yet, what was more

Figure 6.2.
Public/Private Sponsorship of H-Coal

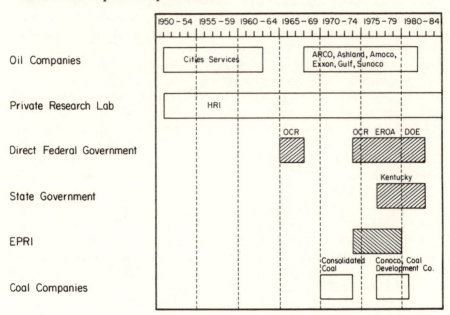

important was the formation of a coalition to back the H-coal technology. A pictorial representation of these sponsors is shown in Fig. 6.2. This coalition of oil and coal companies was solidified after OCR discontinued funding of the PDU in the late 1960s. The group, later to be headed by Ashland, was responsible for proving to the federal government that there was a significant amount of private sector interest in the technology. Unfortunately, as we will discuss below, this coalition broke down prior to the commercialization of H-coal.

TECHNICAL ISSUES

Technically, the scale of possible H-coal production has grown at a constant rate since its inception in the early 1960s. Most of this growth can be attributed to H-coal's champion, HRI. Even when federal funds were scarce, HRI maintained some level of effort in researching and developing H-coal. Primarily, the "emphasis [in developing H-coal] is on process development. . . . Basic science is not perceived to be that significant," according to an HRI expert interviewed for this project. Below, we consider several of the technical issues contributing to H-coal's development. We will focus on four areas: scale-up; project schedule; project management; and the differences in the one-stage versus two-stage technologies.

Scale-Up

Issues surrounding scale-up are always important in first-of-a-kind plants. Scale-up factors for the H-coal process are shown in Fig. 6.3. With the operation of the Catlettsburg Pilot Plant, scale-up to a commercial size plant was greatly minimized. Scale-up factors between the PDU and the pilot plant were 7 (reactor diameter) and 73 (throughput), whereas factors for a 50,000 barrel per day (bpd) plant would be 2.3 (reactor diameter) and 11 (throughput).[16]

For the Breckinridge project, the proposed 50,000 bpd plant would consist of five trains, each of which would have 11 times the throughput of the pilot plant. While this throughput scale-up factor is much lower than in other stages of the research process, it must be remembered that the technology is still first-of-a-kind. Each train is about the same size as the largest commercial analog to H-coal, the H-oil facilities.

However, as an HRI expert interviewed for this project noted, "The

Figure 6.3.
H-Coal Reactor Scale-up Factors

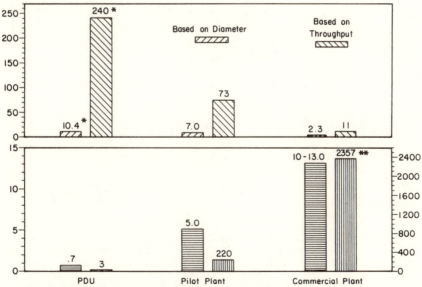

* Represents approximate scale-up between bench-scale and PDU unit.
** Capacity for each of seven on-line reactors.

ebullating bed has lent itself to successful scale-up." Scale-up in the case of H-coal, however, was a potentially significant technical barrier, as was typical of all DCL technologies.

Project Schedule

The second important technical issue concerns the timing of the decision to proceed with construction. By the end of 1976, when ERDA authorized the construction of the plant, only 20 percent of the detailed design had been completed by HRI. It was not until February 1978, some thirteen months into the construction of the plant, that the design work was finished. This overlap is shown in Fig. 6.4. A General Accounting Office (GAO) report, released later in the project, blamed this premature decision to start construction for most of the $120 million cost overruns experienced during the project.[17] In a 1980 letter to the GAO, Charles Hoertz of ASFI noted,

Approximately 25 percent of the 117 million dollar cost increase in the H-Coal project is a direct result of added scope of work. . . . Essentially all of the remaining 75 percent of the 117 million dollars can be attributed to the decision to

Figure 6.4.
Timetable of Project Delays

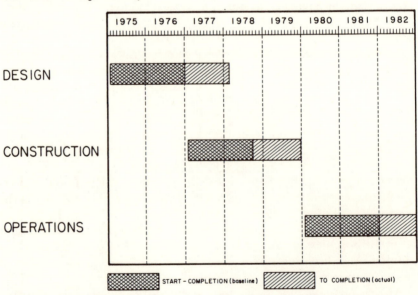

Source: U.S. Congress, General Accounting Office. Controlling Federal Costs for Coal Liquefaction Hinges on Management and Contracting Improvements. Washington, D.C.: U.S. General Printing Office, February 4, 1981.

proceed with construction of the plant with only 20 to 25 percent of the engineering design work completed.[18]

As a result of the cost-sharing ceiling agreement established with the private sponsors, the federal government incurred almost all of the added cost of the project.

Schedule overlap is common in large construction projects. However, in the case of first-of-a-kind technologies, schedule overlap has to be closely monitored.

Project Management

Another important consideration, which we have broadly classified under this section on technical aspects of H-coal, is project management. H-Coal was fortunate in that a relatively large-scale pilot plant had been constructed. It was possible, therefore, to learn from this experience, especially in terms of managing the design, engineering, construction, and management of a first-of-a-kind plant.

Construction of the H-coal pilot plant started in January 1977. ERDA had the ultimate responsibility for the overall execution and management of the project. ASFI was the prime contractor for both the construction and operation phases. ASFI, in turn, contracted with Badger Plants, of Cambridge, Massachusetts for most of the plant construction.

Two key committees were established to oversee and to guide the project. A Management Advisory Committee (MAC) and a Technical Advisory Committee (TAC) were chaired by ERDA and included representatives from each of the private sponsors. The MAC was specifically responsible for:

- policy matters
- key personnel changes
- cost changes exceeding $100,000
- changes in project scope
- schedule changes
- changes in total contract costs
- appointment of members to the TAC

Technical direction was provided by the TAC, which included a mandate to:

- technically evaluate and review plant construction and operation;
- provide technical expertise to the project from member organizations;

- approve or reject technical changes within the scope of the project;
- approve or reject cost changes between $50,000 and $100,000;
- make recommendations to the MAC on project scope.

Another committee, the Technical Review Panel (TRP), was established to make quick recommendations on day-to-day problems and concerns.

A team approach was developed to utilize the expertise of the private participants. Each sponsor was given the option to place people in various positions in the construction and operation management structures. For example, Standard Oil of Indiana filled the engineering manager position and HRI filled the technical manager job.

Throughout the construction and operation phases, many changes in the organizational structure of the project occurred. In addition, key personnel changes were frequent. Figure 6.5 illustrates these fluctuations. On the federal government level, ERDA was reorganized into the Department of Energy (DOE) in October 1977. Management of the project was assigned to the DOE Office of Fossil Energy in Washington, D.C. An inspection of the project in 1978 by the DOE Office of the Inspector General (OIG) resulted in another organization.[19] In February 1980 the Oak Ridge Operations Office of DOE was assigned the responsibility for managerial control of the project.

The prime contractor also varied within and between project phases. HRI was the prime contractor for Phase I, which focused on plant design. ASFI was initially the prime contractor for Phase II. However, a DOE Office of Fossil Energy Assessment in the spring of 1978 found the construction phase of the project "out of control."[20] Consequently, Badger Construction Management replaced Ashland as prime contractor for Phase II on July 12, 1978. Even though ASFI managed plant construction up to July 1978, they cannot be held responsible for all of

Figure 6.5.
Organizational Changes in the H-Coal Project

PHASE	PHASE 1 - DESIGN December 1973-February 1978	PHASE 2 - CONSTRUCTION January 1977-December 1979	PHASE 3 - OPERATIONS January 1980-December 1982
Federal Government Management	• Office of Coal Research Department of Interior (December '73 - October '74) • Fossil Energy Division Energy Research & Dev. Ag. (October '74 - October '77) • Office of Fossil Energy Department of Energy (October '77 - February '78)	• Fossil Energy Division ERDA (January '77 - October '77) • Office of Fossil Energy Department of Energy (October '77 - February '79) • Oak Ridge Operations Office Department of Energy (February '79 - December '79)	• Oak Ridge Operations Office Department of Energy (January '80 - December '82)
Prime Contractor	• Hydrocarbon Research, Inc. (December '73 - February '78)	• Ashland Synthetic Fuels (January '77 - July '78) • Badger Construction Mgmt. (July '78 - December '79)	• Ashland Synthetic Fuels (January '80 - December '82)

the problems during that time period. In fact, a 1977 ASFI report to ERDA cited difficulties with Badger's management practices.[21] The management of plant operations, Phase III, was transferred back to ASFI.

Organizational changes were compounded with personnel changes. A 1981 GAO report found,

the H-Coal project also experienced shifts in key personnel. For example, DOE had three different site project managers, two firms in charge of construction, and six to seven different construction managers all involved during the 36 month H-Coal construction effort.[22]

Furthermore, the quality of the management was questioned by the OIG during their 1978 inspection of the project. The DOE project manager, the only DOE staff person assigned to the on-site DOE office, "did not have training or experience in the management of major construction projects of this type."[23]

Both the 1981 GAO report and the 1978 OIG inspection blame poor management for many of the delays and cost overruns experienced during the project. It is clear that "hand-off failure," that is, the distortion or inefficient transfer of essential project information from one step or group of specialists to another, occurred throughout the project.[24] Certainly one of the contributing factors to the project delays noted in Fig. 6.5 was the large number of actors involved in the project.

The management structure may have also contributed to the delays. The GAO report called the organizational structure "nebulous" with DOE making many of the final decisions after private deliberations.[25] Although the MAC and TAC were established as "advisory" committees, they also made important management decisions like project scope, funding, and personnel. A 1979 Rand report commented on this type of organization:

A committee management system is even more frowned upon in the literature. Timely decisions are particularly important for a project once detailed design has begun and committees are notorious for being unable to make decisions rapidly.[26]

Unfortunately, project management issues are generally not considered to be an important aspect of the development of a technology. However, in the case of H-coal and most other first-of-a-kind DCL technologies, project management becomes a critical factor when it comes time for the process to be demonstrated on a pilot or demonstration plant level.

ECONOMIC ISSUES

Thus far, we have considered that policy and technical issues of consequence in the development of H-coal. Below, we will examine the economic factors that have influenced H-coal's growth. First we will take a look at various estimates of the value of H-coal products versus conventional sources. Then we will discuss the economic reasons for Ashland's decision not to build a commercial plant. Finally, we will examine capital cost estimates for a commercial scale H-coal plant.

Cost Per Barrel Production Cost

Most of the estimates for the cost of a barrel of fuel oil equivalent from an H-coal plant vary tremendously. Expected plant size, type of coal, operation of the plant, detail of the cost estimate, and many other factors influence the value of this number. Given the potential for fluctuation, many analysts view cost per fuel oil equivalent only as a rough estimate of economic viability. Nonetheless, these conventional fuel comparisons have influenced decision making on the development of H-coal. Below, we review several of these studies.

The first estimates of some consequence were made in 1966. The first study was conducted by HRI and showed that a 98,000 barrel per day (bpd) plant would produce a product that would be competitive with gasoline.[27] OCR also contracted with the American Oil Company to provide an independent evaluation of the H-coal process and HRI's economic calculations. American Oil's figures were very close to HRI's estimates. Both groups projected that a large-scale commercial plant could produce gasoline for about 12 cents per gallon. In 1966, this figure would have been competitive with the price of large lots of domestic gasoline sold at the refinery. American went as far as to recommend that a demonstration-scale plant be built and operated.

A second set of estimates was prepared just prior to the construction of the pilot plant. A 1976 study by the Bureau of Mines estimated that a 50,000 barrel per stream day H-coal plant would produce the equivalent of boiler fuel at \$36.63/barrel.[28]

The most recent estimates were made after some experience with the pilot plant and in preparation for the decision to proceed with the Breckinridge plant. Olliver reported the costs to be \$27.50 (1980 dollars) per barrel. These costs include coal (\$11.23/barrel), direct operating costs (\$6.33/barrel), and other fixed costs (\$9.94/barrel).[29] Olliver also estimates capital costs at \$22.70 per barrel, bringing the total cost per barrel to \$50.20. Another estimate in 1981 dollars puts the required selling price of H-coal at \$38.95 per barrel equivalent.

Due to the recent fall in oil prices, the gap between conventional fuels and H-coal products is actually increasing. In part, this gap explains why the private sector has been reluctant to invest in H-coal. In Chapter 7, we will explore this issue in some depth.

Financial Decision to Terminate the Breckinridge Project

Throughout the rocky history of the H-coal pilot plant project, the goal of the research—gaining sufficient knowledge to build a technically and economically viable commercial H-coal facility—was vigorously pursued.

Ashland had been planning for the commercial H-coal facility since 1971, long before the pilot plant was constructed and operated. Ashland's philosophy was simple. With construction costs and inflation escalating rapidly, their goal was to build the commercial plant as quickly as possible. However, in order to minimize the risks associated with building a pioneer commercial plant,[30] Ashland found it necessary to search for partners to share the costs of their commercial venture. With attention focused on the pilot plant in the early 1970s, progress on the commercial plant proceeded slowly.

In 1979, Ashland found its first partner—the Federal Government. A Phase 0 contract of $7.5 million was awarded to ASFI by the newly formed U.S. Department of Energy (DOE). Under this contract, work commenced on process design, cost estimation, economic analysis, and environmental assessment of the commercial plant. AIRCO, a subsidiary of British Oxygen, also joined the partnership. HRI and Bechtel, a large engineering consulting firm, were designated as the main subcontractors for the Phase 0 study.

Compared with the Catlettsburg plant, the commercial plant was a large undertaking. The plant, which was estimated to cost $3 billion in 1980, would produce 50,000 barrels of synthetic oil per day. Over 22,000 tons of coal would be required per day and the plant would employ an average of 5000 construction workers and 1500 employees to operate the plant.

Another partner, the Commonwealth of Kentucky, provided some incentives to the project that ensured its siting in Kentucky. First, the Kentucky Department of Energy (KDOE) acquired a 1600-acre plot of land forty-five miles southwest of Louisville in Breckinridge County. The Commonwealth paid over $2.5 million in 1980 for a four-year option on the site. Additionally, through a contract with the University of Kentucky's Institute for Mining and Minerals Research, KDOE offered process development testing and research support.

On the federal level, some important changes were being made in energy policy. The Synthetic Fuels Corporation (SFC) was formed in 1980 in response to the 1979 oil shortages and with hopes of achieving energy self-efficiency.[31] Congress allocated $17 billion to the SFC to be distributed in the form of financial incentives (loans, loan guarantees, price supports, etc.) to demonstration and commercial synthetic fuel projects. With Phase 0 completed in 1981, ASFI immediately applied for a 3 billion dollar loan guarantee from the SFC for the Breckinridge project.

Suddenly, in the fall of 1981, enthusiasm for the H-coal project began to dwindle. On the world market, a "glut" of oil appeared and oil prices, which had skyrocketed in recent months, began to stabilize. The urgency to commercialize synthetic fuels slowly started to dissipate. AIRCO backed out of the partnership in February 1982, citing high capital costs and the lack of other risk-sharing partners as its reasons. Ashland, however, remained committed to the project. Paul Chellgren, senior vice-president for Ashland Oil, noted at their annual meeting:

While costs and uncertainties of developing a commercial synfuels industry are staggering, we continue to believe that developing this capability is a valuable security for America.[32]

As oil prices remained constant or decreased and construction costs continued to rise, Ashland bowed to the pressures of the economy and scaled down the size of their plant. The plant size was cut in half, from an output of 50,000 barrels per day to 25,000 barrels per day. Although this action lowered the cost of the project, the price still remained in the billions of dollars.

Ashland vigorously continued to pursue additional partners. The U.S. Synthetic Fuels Corporation announced on June 18, 1982, that the Breckinridge project was one of the two projects (out of sixty-three considered) that was advancing to the final stage of consideration for financial assistance. Without the SFC support and additional sponsors, the project would certainly collapse. Ashland was given a September 1, 1982, deadline by the SFC to line up adequate equity for the project. At this point, Bechtel was the only other partner in the consortium—at least five to six other companies would be needed to meet the deadline.[33] Fearful that the project would be cancelled, the Commonwealth of Kentucky donated an additional $1 million to the project in July 1982, Also, ASFI was in partnership negotiations with Ruhrkohle, A.G., a West German firm that had joined the pilot plant consortium in 1978.

By September 1 Ashland had not attracted any additional partners. The SFC extended the deadline, allowing Ashland to put together its financial package by the end of November. On November 23, 1982, the headlines for the Louisville Courier Journal read, "Ashland Oil Kills Plan for Synthetic Fuel Plant in Breckinridge County." John R. Hall,

Chief Executive Officer of Ashland Oil, cited the uncertainty of future crude oil prices in the volatile world market, the massive capital investment, and the reduction in potential tax benefits as the reasons for Ashland's decision to drop the project. Ashland had invested $7.5 million in the project and Bechtel $1.5 million. Hall concluded that "If we rely on the free market with only limited government assistance, synthetic fuels may not be available in the next crisis when they will be badly needed."[34] Bechtel resubmitted the Breckinridge project in the third SFC solicitation. However, the project was again rejected by the SFC due to insufficient equity participation.

The ultimate decision not to commercialize the H-coal technology was justified on economic grounds by Ashland. And without Ashland, the project was doomed. As an AIRCO official later commented, "Ashland is pretty crucial to the project."[35]

Plant Capital Estimates

Since the "massive capital investment necessary"[36] for the Breckinridge plant was cited a major reason for dropping the project, it may be instructive to take a closer look at the expected capital costs for the proposed Breckinridge plant.[37] The total capital costs for the 50,000 bpd plant were estimated to be $3.258 billion (January 1981 dollars).[38] Bechtel/Ashland believe that the capital estimate is accurate within a range of +19 to −17 percent. This estimate includes a contingency allowance of 15 percent of the subtotal plant costs.

While the Ashland/Bechtel estimates were made in good faith, it is reasonable to assume that these figures are severely underestimated. The Rand Corporation, in a comprehensive study of more than forty first-of-a-kind process plants, found capital costs to be grossly understated for these projects.[39] If we apply the Rand methodology to the estimate provided by Ashland/Bechtel, we come up with a much larger capital cost estimate. The Rand equation for estimating cost growth based on their evaluation of forty first-of-a-kind plants is:

$$
\begin{aligned}
\text{Cost Growth} = 1.122 \ &-0.00297 \times \text{PCTNEW} \\
&-0.0213 \times \text{IMPURITIES} \\
&-0.0114 \times \text{COMPLEXITY} \\
&+0.00111 \times \text{INCLUSIVENESS} \\
&-0.0401 \times \text{PROJECT DEFINITION}
\end{aligned}
$$

$R^2 = 0.83$

Standard error of the estimate = 0.083

where the variables in the above equation have the following definitions:

PCTNEW: Percent of estimate incorporating technology unproven in commercial use.

IMPURITIES: Assessment by industry process engineers of difficulties with process impurities encountered during development.

COMPLEXITY: Block count of all process steps in plant.

INCLUSIVENESS: Derived from checklist measuring completeness of estimate (percent of items included).

PROJECT DEFINITION: Levels of site-specific information and engineering included in estimate.

COST GROWTH: Ratio of estimated to actual costs, excluding external cost factors.

The following values were assigned to these variables after consulting with experts at the Rand Corporation and after reviewing the feasibility studies prepared for the Breckinridge project:

PCTNEW = 28.1. A detailed cost estimate completed for the Breckinridge project showed that 28.1 percent of the capital costs can be attributed to the coal slurry unit, the gasifier, and the liquefaction reactor.

IMPURITIES = 3. Severe impurity problems occurred during the operation of the Catlettsburg project. While many of these problems have been fixed, the Rand model is based on impurity problems during process development.

COMPLEXITY = 17. The block count for the plant is presented in a Mitre report.[40]

INCLUSIVENESS = 100. The Breckinridge estimate was all inclusive.

PROJECT DEFINITION = 4.5. This figure is a compilation of values related to the degree of definition of the unit configurations, soils and hydrology, environment, health, and engineering.

Given these assumptions, the cost growth factor the Rand model predicts is 0.711393. When the reciprocal of this factor, 1.4057, is multiplied by the best available cost estimate, it represents the likely cost of the project. A comparison of these estimates is shown in Fig. 6.6.

If the pilot plant is any indication of the problem of estimating project capital costs, then the Rand figure presented above may be more accurate than the Ashland/Bechtel estimates. Project costs for the pilot plant soared during the construction and operation phases. Fig. 6.7 presents a plot of the expected completion costs at the time the estimate was made. Taking the first capital cost estimate made in mid-1976 and comparing it with the actual cost, the cost growth is relatively large.

In addition to improper management, other factors led to cost overruns. ASFI was severely criticized by GAO and OIG for authorizing the construction of a permanent administration building and guard change

Figure 6.6.
Capital Cost Estimates for the Breckinridge Plant (50,000 bpd, 1981 Dollars)

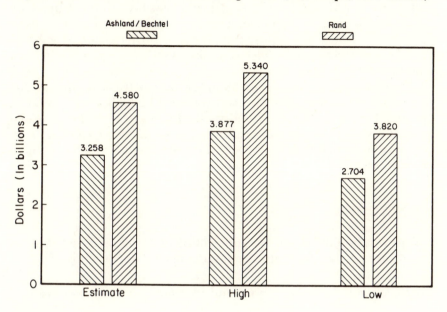

Figure 6.7.
Baseline Estimates of Total Project Costs

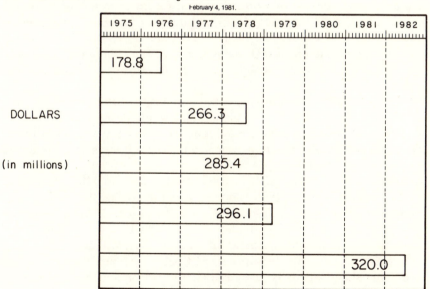

Source: U.S. Congress, General Accounting Office. Controlling Federal Costs for Coal Liquefaction Hinges on Management and Contracting Improvements. Washington, D.C.: U.S. General Printing Office, February 4, 1981.

house at a cost of over $1 million. Ashland has since offered to purchase these buildings at the completion of the project.[41] DOE procurement policies and failure to prioritize equipment and material purchases based on the construction schedule were also cited as contributing to cost increases.[42]

Plant costs also are a consideration for the newer CTSL process. According to an expert at HRI, plant costs will be higher for the CTSL process but "increased yield and product quality offset the increased capital costs." This remark is particularly troublesome given the reluctance of investors to support DCL commercialization due to the high capital costs.

CONCLUSIONS

While conclusions on the development of DCL will be included in the final chapter, the above discussion raises several important issues:

1. Is government support necessary if H-coal is to become a commercial technology?

H-Coal flourished under government sponsorship and has floundered as a purely private initiative. An expert interviewed for this project concluded, "HRI believes there is still a need for government support and involvement. A $30/bbl oil price would not be a sufficient guarantee to cause private investment in DCL." Economically, H-coal is not competitive under current market conditions. In the short term, commercialization will not occur without some financial support from government.

Another concern with H-coal is the immensity of the capital requirement needed for a commercial plant. Some would term a commercial H-coal plant a "mega" project. Investments on such a large scale with only marginal and highly risky returns will not occur without some support of the federal government.

As recently as 1985, DOE invested $4.3 million in HRI's two-stage CTSL process. The *Oil Daily* reported that the goal of the project is to "improve the overall economics of synthetics fuels."[43] What happens several years down the road when the process is not yet competitive enough for the private sector to adopt and also too close to commercialization for government support? H-Coal is currently trapped in this economic stalemate. It is possible that the two-stage CTSL process is destined to meet the same fate.

2. What technical developments will promote/hinder the commercialization of H-coal?

Little basic science research was pursued by HRI and the focus of most government funding was in preparing the process for commercialization. The aim of much of the research was to produce a coal-based product that was economically competitive. Obviously, this strategy failed. Since so many other economic factors influence the competitiveness of H-coal, a technological fix on the economic viability of the product is a tenuous goal.

3. What political coalitions are necessary for the continued development of H-coal?

The coalition formed to support H-coal in the 1970s has dissolved. Without this coalition of private and public sponsors, it is unlikely that H-coal will move into commercialization. The primary reason given by most of the members in the coalition for leaving the partnership was the questionable economics of the process. For many participants, there was not even a slight chance of a reasonable return on their investment dollars.

4. What lessons can be learned from the Catlettsburg experience?

One of the most important lessons to be learned from the Catlettsburg pilot plant is the effective management of jointly sponsored first-of-a-kind synfuel plants. It is our speculation that the turbulent Catlettsburg management environment soured many of the participants' interest in a commercial scale effort. An Ashland Oil official interviewed for this project best expressed the sentiment of everyone involved in H-coal: "We are taking a 'do nothing' attitude. Until the economics change, we will not do anything."

7 —————————— AN ECONOMICS-DRIVEN PERSPECTIVE ON DIRECT COAL LIQUEFACTION

Throughout the history of DCL development, the albatross around its neck has been the price of oil. The price of oil has come to be the standard by which alternative energy sources are compared and, by this criterion, DCL has been and continues to be a bust. When industry and policymakers dismiss DCL as "not competitive," they usually mean that it is not competitive with prevailing costs of oil.

During many periods, there has been a "light at the end of the tunnel" syndrome concerning assessments of the competitiveness of DCL with respect to the price of oil. Consider the admonition of Rep. Wayne Aspinall (Dem., Colorado) at a May 1969 briefing session with the director of the Office of Coal Research. Responding to Director George Fumich's optimistic assessment of the competitiveness of the OCR-sponsored coal liquefaction project, Aspinall cautioned:

if you are not careful you are going to get yourself in the same position as . . . the Bureau of Mines was, because 10–15 years ago they kept saying, "We are within a half cent, and if you will just give us some money, why we will be competitive."[1]

There are many explanations of the inability of synfuels and DCL to compete and this chapter, and other portions of this analysis, are concerned with the issue of the economic competitiveness of DCL. Arguably, DCL will not flourish until such a time that it can be demonstrated to be competitive. Thus, it is worth considering some of the estimates of the relative competitiveness of DCL and the assumptions that underpin those estimates. After presenting this evidence, the next section retreats from this hard line and makes the point that the competitiveness criterion may not be as clear-cut as it might seem.

THE FAILURE OF DCL TO COMPETE: ESTIMATES AND EXPLANATIONS

Given the limited experience with "commercial" DCL in the United States, all of the price estimates for DCL products are based on forecasts. Many of these estimates compare projected prices for coal liquids with 1986/87 petroleum prices. An approach favored by many analysts is to develop a base case production plant and then calculate the price per barrel of the DCL product that would make the plant competitive. A variation of this approach, which evaluates seven major DCL technologies is shown in Fig. 7.1.

Historically, price comparisons of conventional fuels versus synthetic fuels derived from DCL have shown that, at best, DCL is marginally competitive. Most economic assessments have found DCL fuels to be more costly than comparable conventional fuels.

One theory suggests that DCL will never be competitive with conventional fuels.[2] The reasoning is that the inputs to a DCL commercialization effort are fueled by conventional sources. Through complex energy input/output analysis, the CRS report showed that the price of DCL products will have to be higher than the costs of the conventional fuels

Figure 7.1.
Required Selling Price* (Relative to the Projected Price of Lummus ITSL Product)

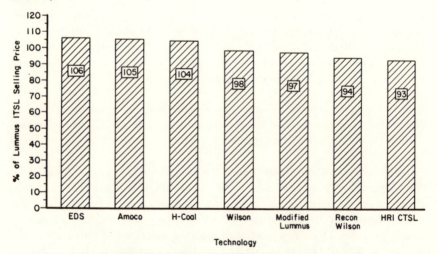

* Based on a plant size using 30,000 tons/day of dry coal.

Source: Sawy, Gray, Tallb, & Tomlinson, June 1986

Table 7.1.
H-Coal Process Economic Projections

	Oil Price ($ / Bbl)				
	9	30	50	75	100
CAPITAL INVESTMENT - MM$					
Plant Facilities	875	1,430	1,768	2,033	2,245
Other	98	160	197	227	250
TOTAL	973	1,590	1,965	2,260	2,495
OPERATING EXPENSES - MM$/year					
Coal	82	233	295	357	391
Water	2	3	3	4	4
Cat., Chem., Etc.	41	71	82	89	96
Labor & Sup.	43	59	66	71	76
Fixed Costs	42	69	85	98	108
TOTAL	210	435	531	619	675
FINANCING (100% Eq.) - MM$/yr.					
Depreciation	44	72	88	102	112
Equity Recovery	117	278	393	509	624
Fed. Income Tax	108	257	363	470	576
TOTAL	269	607	844	1,081	1,312
Total Rev. Req.	479	1,042	1,375	1,700	1,987
By-Prod. Credit,	27	38	49	61	74
SYNFUEL REV. REQ.	452	1,004	1,326	1,639	1,913
$/Barrel	27.82	61.78	81.60	100.86	117.72
$/MMBtu	4.85	10.75	14.20	17.55	20.49
FINANCING (50% Eq.) - MM$/yr.					
Depreciation	44	72	88	102	112
Debt. Reduction	34	80	123	170	212
Equity Recovery	58	139	197	254	312
Fed. Income Tax	54	128	182	234	288
TOTAL	190	419	590	760	924
Total Rev. Required	400	854	1,121	1,379	1,599
By-Prod. Credit	27	38	49	61	74
SYNFUEL REV. REQ.	373	816	1,072	1,318	1,525
$/Barrel	22.95	50.22	65.97	81.11	93.85
$/MMBtu	4.00	8.74	11.48	14.11	16.33

Source: Costs of Synthetic Fuels in Relation to Oil Prices., Subcommittee on Energy Development and Applications of The Committee on Science and Technology, U.S. House of Representatives, Ninety-Seventh Congress, U.S. Government Printing Office, Washington (1981), p. 64.

that are used to construct the plants, produce the materials, and operate the facilities. In times of higher energy costs, the costs of input to a plant increase at a rate that generally discourages investments. When energy costs are low, DCL plants cannot be justified because of the decreased value of energy products. As illustrated for the H-coal base case in Table 7.1, there is a small window of opportunity for DCL development.

One of the experts interviewed expressed a typical view on the input/output problem: "Synthetic liquids continue to sit at 1.5 to 2 times the price of the same products produced from oil no matter what happens to the world oil price. The basic problem is that coal is a solid and needs to be converted to a liquid."

Another Look at the Competitiveness Criterion

It is difficult to overemphasize the importance of price comparisons with oil to the development fate of DCL. The prime importance of this criterion is taken as a guiding assumption in this economic analysis. Nevertheless, the competitiveness criterion, despite its importance, is neither as uncomplicated nor as final as might appear to be the case. There are three major points to be remembered: (1) statements on competitiveness are essentially speculative; (2) other suitable criteria may be envisioned; (3) relying on the price of oil as the chief indicator of competitiveness introduces a sometimes undesirable wild card into policy deliberations and business projections.

Competitiveness Judgments are Speculative

Clearly, the best available evidence indicates that DCL is not currently competitive with the price of oil. However, it is worth bearing in mind that any claim about competitiveness is, for one very good reason, speculative. That reason: no U.S. DCL plant has gone from pilot to commercial stage. Thus, arguments about competitiveness are saying, for all intents and purposes, if there were a full-scale commercial plant, then it would not be competitive. Such speculative claims seem to be based on sound reasoning but it is nevertheless worthwhile to underscore that estimates are not the same as hard data.

Input/output explanations notwithstanding,[3] it is certainly not the case that synfuels are, under current real world conditions, inevitably noncompetitive. The success of South Africa's SASOL projects indicates that it is possible to develop synfuel alternatives that are competitive, given certain conditions. The energy picture in South Africa is markedly different from the United States—no indigenous petroleum, minimal environmental standards, cheap labor—but there is one distinctive feature of the South African context that has particular relevance to the U.S. case: South Africa has had a long-term commitment to a single class of viable technology, with the result that dividends have already been seen.[4] Perhaps what has been learned is not that DCL is inexorably noncompetitive but that it is competitive only with careful nurturing and commitment.

Alternative Criteria

Competitiveness with the price of oil is such a pervasive and obviously important criterion that it is easy to forget other standards for measuring the returns from DCL investment. Two alternative criteria warrant brief mention, a third warrants more detailed discussion.

National Security

With the breakdown of OPEC and the reduction of lines at gas stations, the national security criterion for DCL looms as less apparent. Yet one could argue that competitiveness with the price of oil is a poor measure of viability when evaluating energy alternatives from a national security standpoint. The early German advances in DCL were chiefly motivated by national security, the South African venture has a similar national security motivation and, periodically, the U.S. investment in DCL and other synfuels has been rationalized along the lines of national security.

As late as 1979, the national security argument for U.S. development of synfuels still had much support. In testimony before the U.S. Senate's Governmental Affairs Committee, Paul Ignatius, Eugene Zuckert, and Lloyd Cutler, all former public officials in Defense or National Security, staunchly defended the need for the Synfuels Corporation with allusions to Pearl Harbor, the shortages during the Korean War, and, of course, the threat of OPEC.[5]

Concern with the national security rationale for U.S. investment in synfuels did not originate in the 1970s. Consider the testimony of Secretary of Interior Harold Ickes on legislation leading to the earliest U.S. synfuel investments:

A sudden cessation or curtailment of petroleum and its products would dislodge and upset the system to which we have become accustomed. . . . No man can predict the vast ramifications that would result from a cutting off of gasoline and oil [but] it would be of momentous consequence attended by a possible decline in world power and prestige.[6]

The point is simple. National security changes the nature of economic assessment such that the normal rules go out the window. To the extent that national security is a significant justification for DCL investment, the traditional competitiveness criterion is less meaningful. Presently, the national security rationale is not in favor in the United States. But this could change quickly, sweeping away concerns about the industry's return on investment.[7] To put it another way, the Manhattan Project, the Apollo Project, and the Strategic Defense Initiative were (are) not "competitive," and the German synfuel effort before and during World War II carried with it no assumptions about competitiveness.

Clean Fuel and Competitiveness

Another issue that complicates assessing competitiveness is that one must consider the implicit standard of fuel quality and cleanliness involved. If the demand is for an extremely clean product then the competitiveness equation is altered. In the words of one of the interviewees in this analysis: "If you look at the objective of coal liquefaction to be to produce a clean coal product (low sulphur, low nitrogen, low ash), then it would be very difficult for DCL to compete as a boiler fuel when it comes in with a price of about $50/bbl, about $10 per million Btu's. With the price of coal as a utility boiler fuel at about $2/million Btu's, there is no present interest in DCL as a source."

Clearly, a change in environmental quality standards could drastically alter the competitiveness of DCL with coal. For example, tough new anti-acid rain legislation might vault DCL to a new level of competitiveness.

Extending Knowledge of DCL

Many observers feel that DCL has emerged more from craft engineering, even trial and error, than from science. One of the experts contributing to this analysis contends that "coal science adds little; engineering ingenuity is what has been and is needed . . . fundamental understanding of process technology, basic science, has followed new developments rather than leading them." But whether DCL progresses from basic science, engineering, or even serendipity, the basic point is that knowledge development is irrelevant (except indirectly) to the competitiveness criterion. It must be underscored that if DCL research is abandoned because DCL processes are not competitive, the likelihood of achieving the breakthroughs (especially technological and engineering breakthroughs) that might lead to greater efficiency is obviously diminished. The "it's not competitive" argument is in a sense self-defeating.

This is not to say that there is reason to encourage sending good money after bad. Some DCL processes have been given rather substantial tests and for one reason or another have fallen aside. But others cannot be said to have been tested to the extent that the conclusions about noncompetitiveness are clear. Moreover, there is some value to the learning that DCL research permits and, from that standpoint, it seems sensible to view at least some percentage of DCL expenditure as a fixed overhead investment.

Regional Economic Impact and DCL Development

As essentially an aside during hearings concerning OCR funding, Rep. Ed Edmondson (Dem., Oklahoma) tendered his support but complained that despite "doing all I could do to increase authorizations, I still have not seen a project started in my state, although we have substantial coal reserves and have submitted projects. It is kind of discouraging."[8] This mild expression of disappointment epitomizes an aspect of synfuels development that has little to do with traditional notions about competitiveness with oil. Synfuels projects and DCL are prized (by Congress, at least) as much for their regional economic impact as for their possible contribution to energy supplies. As the Edmondson anecdote suggests, there is nothing untoward about this desire for an infusion of economic resources into one's region, and the desire need not take precedence over other broader policy concerns (Edmondson did not, in a fit of pique, withdraw his support from synfuels development).

Regional economic concerns have always been an important supplemental economic rationale in synfuels projects. The earliest U.S. policies for synfuels research included some attention to regional and other indirect impacts of technology and this concern has been sustained up to the zenith period of synfuel support. As late as October 1979, the associate director of the Office and Management and Budget was telling the Senate Subcommittee on Energy and Power that 90,000 jobs would be created by a fully funded synfuels corporation; estimates for these jobs were for 20,000 in coal production, 64,000 in synthetic fuel plants, and 11,000 in the shale oil industry.[9] Any economic assessment of the development of DCL that neglects the secondary economic rationales pertaining to regional impact is less than complete.

Estimates of the broad-based impact of a synfuels corporation necessarily involved dubious assumptions and soft numbers. To get some insight into the magnitude of regional effects it is helpful to consider one of the more careful and systematic projections of regional impacts, an analysis of projected impact of synfuel construction on the western Kentucky region.[10] The 1982 base-year projections for the western Kentucky region assumed that before 1992 as many as five new synthetic fuel plants would be built, supplementing the four already under construction. Synfuel plants included Tri-State and W.R. Grace (both Henderson County), SRC I&II (adjacent Davies County), and H-Coal (Breckinridge County). To get some notion of the anticipated magnitude of the energy construction efforts, it is worth noting that projections called for a peak labor force of 27,000, plus 8000 personnel to manage and operate the plants. In Breckinridge and Davies Counties alone it was projected that some 14,000 additional commuters and relocators could be anticipated for 1987. Projections for the construction workforces included new jobs for a wide variety of workers including boilermakers, carpenters, electricians, iron workers, millwrights, and pipefitters (the latter category comprising 40 percent of the construction labor requirements for the synfuels projects).[11] Such intense demographic impacts have implications that are far-reaching, especially if one considers that these changes are in rural areas with low population density. Jobs are created for local residents, jobs attract new residents, and the influx of new workers has wave effects creating new business. In small counties the multiplier effects can be enormous.[12] It is understandable that members of Congress from underdeveloped and largely rural states might be eager to court synfuels construction projects even if there seems no great prospect for scale-up and competitiveness.

MACROECONOMICS AND DCL INVESTMENT DECISIONS

The previous section called attention to the limitations of the dominant economic criterion for gauging DCL development progress, its cost in relation to the price of oil. While it seems valid to call attention to alternative criteria and the speculative nature of assessments of competitiveness, the plain and simple truth is that the DCL policy effort can best be understood, for better or worse, as a continuing effort to develop a synfuels–DCL industry by making DCL—through one mechanism or another—an attractive investment for business. So long as petroleum is readily available, requires less start-up capital costs, and relies on the areas of traditional expertise of energy companies—drilling, refining, distribution of petroleum products—DCL is a less attractive proposition. If DCL is not believed to be competitive with oil, there is, ceteris paribus, little reason to believe that industry will be anxious to bear additional risk. Even if the estimates of cost comparison are for the most part speculative, the attitude is: Why spend the money to prove that what we suspect is a bad investment is, indeed, a bad investment?

Beginning with the assumption that DCL has never been a sufficiently attractive economic proposition to entice large-scale business investment, it is still possible to consider the impacts of changes in general economic conditions on DCL investment decisions. The fact that those decisions are quite responsive to shifts in policy somewhat clouds the picture, but general economic conditions and industry economics seem to play an independent role as well. In this section, each of a variety of general economic variables is considered in connecting with apparent impacts on DCL investment; the historical events surrounding economic change are "controlled for" by simply recognizing their effects on economic time series. Among the factors considered here are interest rates and inflation, economic stability, and the price of oil. These factors are not considered in depth because few of their effects are specific to DCL investment. Still, they are important enough to warrant identification and modest discussion. In subsequent sections, industry-specific economics and DCL economics are considered. These factors, more specific to context, are considered in greater depth.

The Pivotal Role of Inflation

Fig. 7.2 gives the rate of inflation, as measured by the consumer price index, for the period 1962 to 1985. Both the index and the percent change figures are given. What stands out is that the period 1973–1980 was a period of extraordinary growth in the rate of inflation. It is generally recognized that the unfortunate chronology by which the largest synfuels development push was occurring at the same time as the infla-

Figure 7.2.
Rate of Inflation: CPI*

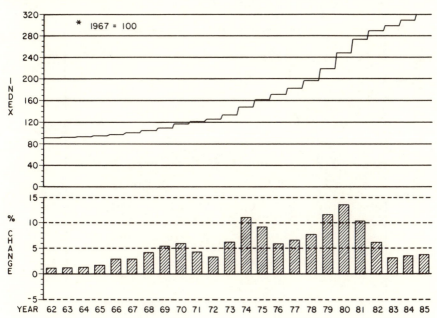

tion rate was soaring had ill effects on investment calculations and, ultimately, DCL development.

As inflation became rampant, industries' approaches to calculating investment decisions had to be changed. Investors who only a few years before had gladly accepted a 4 percent return on bonds now required 9–10 percent. Entrepreneurs who in the early 1960s would have been satisfied with a 10 percent return on investment (ROI) now balked at less than 15–20 percent. At the same time, changes in the tax code were so conservative as to, in many instances, tax purely inflationary "profits." As a result, capital investment projects had to be extraordinarily attractive to warrant risks that seemed much greater than before. One apparent short-term solution, higher-leveraged financing, was not attractive to petroleum companies so long as they viewed investment in their principal line of business as the point of comparison. Fig. 7.3, adapted from Brown and Kahn,[13] depicts conventional calculation of required prices assuming a 7 percent rate of inflation. This figure indicates that conservative financing decisions, requiring early pay-back and early profit, would mitigate strongly against DCL investment during periods of inflation. However, even during high inflation periods, calculations considering streams of benefit, declining capital costs, and discounting make investment a more attractive proposition. Thus, while inflation is, from

Figure 7.3.
Conventional Calculation of Required Synthetic Oil Prices (Expressed in *Constant* Dollars, Assuming a 7% Inflation)

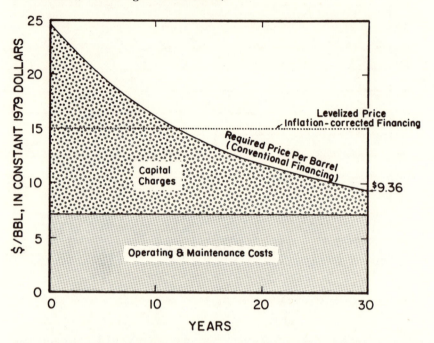

Source: William M. Brown and Herman Kahn, "Prices of Synthetic Fuels: Can They Now Be Competitive," Hudson Institute.

an investment calculation standpoint, a significant disincentive, it should not, in and of itself, be sufficient to preclude investment among stable, well-capitalized firms. It is not inflation alone that deters investment, but inflation in connection with uncertainty and economic instability.

Risk, Uncertainty, and the Price of Oil

In casual conversation risk and uncertainty are often viewed as essentially the same; but not by investors. By its very nature, entrepreneurial activity involves risk—the wagering of scarce resources in hopes of obtaining additional resources; but entrepreneurs prefer to operate in an environment where the extent of risk is known and where the parameters impinging on risk are well established. With high degrees of uncertainty, risk is difficult to calculate and to hedge against.

One of the prime factors exacerbating risk in DCL investment is the uncertainty that flows from that standard measure of competitiveness, the price of oil. The price of oil is sensitive not only to a wide variety of economic factors but, increasingly, political factors as well. The interaction of these political and economic factors complicates cost calculations to such a degree that formal econometric forecasts as to the price of oil are only slightly more valid than the everyday citizen's seat-of-the-pants claim. When this political–economic cloudiness is taken together with technical elements (emergence of new drilling techniques, knowledge of the extent of in-ground petroleum), the price of oil makes investment equations under-determined. Even in recent stable times the price per barrel of oil fluctuates markedly in a quarterly period (see Fig. 7.4, which gives the price per barrel for March–August 1986). Likewise, even short-term forecasts for relatively stable periods include a large range between low and high projections (see Fig. 7.5). As further evidence of the inherent instability accruing from the cost of oil, consider fluctuations in the average retail selling prices for gasoline and residential heating oil for the period 1984–1986 (Fig. 7.6)—again, a relatively stable period and significant variation (even after seasonal adjustments).

A more complete picture of the fluctuations in the price of oil is given in Fig. 7.7, which provides time-series data not only on the price of oil but also on crude oil imports and number of oil wells drilled. A cursory examination of Fig. 7.7 leads to a number of conclusions. In the first place, the year-to-year swing in the price of oil defies any linear regression line; a least-squares prediction of the price of oil would be virtually

Figure 7.4.
Price per Barrel of Oil by Month

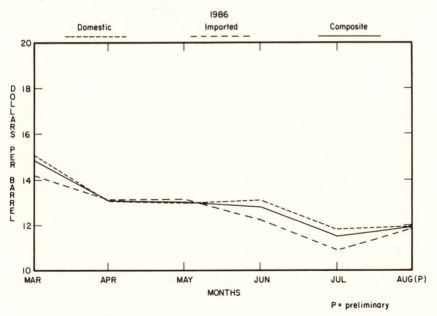

P = preliminary

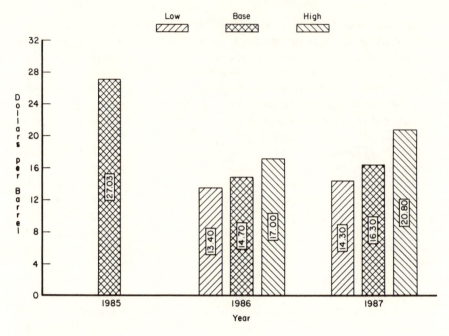

Figure 7.5.
Projected Price per Barrel of Oil: 1985–1987

useless. Business investors, who understand linear change even when it is not in the hoped-for direction, balk at any time series that is (1) not amenable to smoothing and (2) not absolutely vital to investment decisions.[14] Another obvious but nonetheless interesting observation is the limited co-variance between the price data and the import data. This implies that the elasticities of oil demand are large and that demand is poorly predicted by price. By the same token, the number of oil wells drilled is not well predicted by either demand or price variables. What this implies is that critical variables in investment decisions are minimally interrelated (at least at current thresholds) and this complicates the task of the forecaster enormously. When one considers that these critical indicators are explained by separate sets of exogenous variables and that each is subject to intense interaction with policy change variables (e.g., import tax changes, interruptions in supply) and technological variables (i.e., innovations in both extraction/production and application), only one conclusion presents itself: any business venture, including DCL, that takes the price of oil as a benchmark is inexorably fraught with both uncertainty and, in the absence of a risk-bearing surrogate (such as government loan guarantees), a high level of endemic risk. Thus, it is not relatively favorable economic conditions that drive DCL development (positively), it is economic uncertainty (which mitigates against develop-

Figure 7.6.
Average Retail Selling Prices: Motor Gasoline and Residential Heating Oil

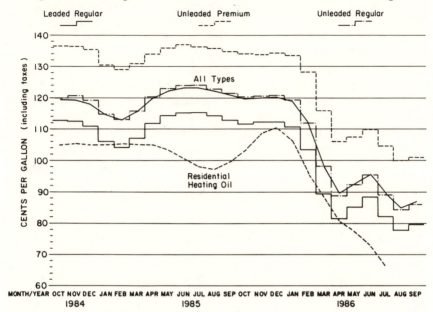

Figure 7.7.
Price of Oil, Crude Oil Imports, and Number of Oil Wells Drilled: 1970–1986

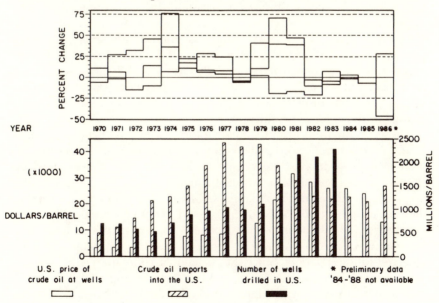

Sources: Statistical Abstract of the U.S.; Monthly Energy Review.

ment). Moreover, while economic favorableness is likely to change dramatically over time, there is no reason to believe that the effects of the price of oil on economic uncertainty are likely to change significantly.

The result of this environment is that DCL is an inherently risky proposition under virtually any macroeconomic scenario. Take for example the H-Coal baseline case. Ashland's Breckinridge H-Coal plant was closed not because of current or projected crude oil prices but because of uncertainty. According to a report at the time, "The firm said in a statement that the uncertainty of further world crude prices and tax law changes have reduced the potential benefits of such a project."[15] That is, the inherent uncertainty interacted dynamically with a change in policy to alter the investment equation. This example is only one of many such in the history of DCL non-development.

INDUSTRY ECONOMICS AND DCL INVESTMENT DECISIONS

The two industries most relevant to DCL development have their share of economic problems. The source and causes of current problems are a matter of some dispute, but neither the coal nor the petroleum industry is currently in a favorable position with respect to debt or investment capital. To some extent, current woes are a function of general economic conditions; to some extent they reflect bad business policy decisions. In order to understand the impact of economic change on DCL production it is useful to provide an historical snapshot of the economics of the two industries.

One indicator of the vitality of the coal and oil industries is the price for fuel delivered to utilities. The price of oil has sharply declined in the past two years and has stayed essentially flat for coal. Utility use accounts for 80 percent of coal consumption and, as one industrial analysis indicates, "the coal industry will mark time in 1986, experiencing scant change in demand or production."[16]

The oil companies are in similar doldrums, in part because of debt. This debt has much to do with recent merger and acquisition strategies (and strategies for avoiding takeover). Restructuring has involved exchange of cash and debt securities for equity securities. By this means, major corporations such as Atlantic Richfield and Phillips have leveraged their balance sheets and shrunk their equity base to reduce the likelihood of takeover. The same approach has been used in takeovers (e.g., Texaco–Getty, Chevron–Gulf). The result is that the oil companies have incurred substantial debt. Since they are public companies with concerns about providing stock dividends, the high debt ratio, when taken with the need to provide a dividend, markedly limits capital available for investment. The decline in the number of wells drilled from 1981 to

1983 is a function of many variables but it is also coincident with changes in the debt postures of major corporations. Moreover, in the absence of strong government-provided incentives (or mandates), investment in oil drilling is, in all likelihood, a major component of investment decisions in DCL.

In the case of coal companies, DCL projects are not, as with the oil companies, subject to approach/avoidance decision conflict. The coal companies might benefit substantially from DCL but simply are too undercapitalized to bear any significant risk. Indeed, even with others bearing much of the risk, the coal companies are simply so undercapitalized that any new project not relying heavily on existing input factors is unworkable even with very short pay-back periods. The reason is illustrated in Fig. 7.8, which gives the profit margin percentages for oil companies and coal companies for the period 1967–1985. The coal companies' profit margins plunged from 27.6 percent in 1976 to about 8 percent in 1978, and then smoothed out at this low level, a level that is a modern industry low. Whatever the promise of synfuels as "welfare for the coal industry," the truth is that the short-lived synfuel programs seem to have had negligible effects on the profit margins of the coal industry.

The discussion above is based on inferences from trend data. However

Figure 7.8.
Profit Margin (%)

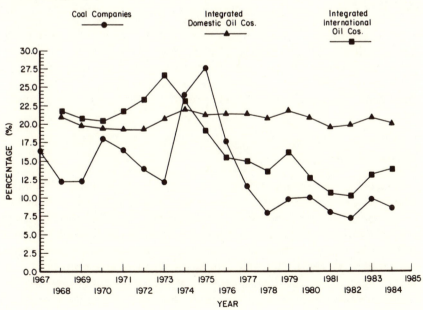

there are some complementary survey-based data supporting the suppositions presented above. In a study asking twenty-one large energy R&D investors about synfuels R&D plans, only 10 percent indicated that they planned to increase R&D and 75 percent indicated either that reductions in synfuels R&D were likely or that future plans were uncertain. More than 80 percent cited unfavorable market conditions as a major factor influencing their synfuels R&D decisions.[17] While these findings are not sufficiently detailed to shed much light on the role of the economic factors discussed above, it does appear that the expectation that synfuels investments will continue to decline if not propped up by government incentives is a realistic expectation. This view is supported by one of the interviewees for this project, who contends "there is no justification for corporate support. Energy companies are in trouble with a surplus of their primary product and [for this reason] industrial efforts are at the monitoring level."

In these last two sections, there has been an attempt to provide some insight into the external economic factors that seem to influence DCL investment decisions. But in addition to the exogenous influences and industry-level effects discussed above, the very tangible economics of plant construction, maintenance, and return play a central and more direct role. The "microeconomics" of DCL decision making are discussed in the next section.

THE ECONOMICS OF FIRM-LEVEL DCL DECISION MAKING

In the previous sections, the macro-level economic factors for DCL commercialization were considered. This section will focus on the firm-level investment decision in DCL and the variety of concerns that are raised during this process. The firm level considerations can be categorized into three main areas: cost growth, performance, and return on investment (ROI).

Cost Growth

Pioneering process plants generally suffer from poor cost estimates. The total cost of designing, constructing, and starting-up a plant are usually greater than predicted. When the estimates do not reflect the final cost, firm officials are forced to scrape up additional funding. In the 1960s and 1970s, many of these cost overruns were covered by the federal government. In the 1980s, however, stringent caps have been placed on government funding, which places the risk of investment back on the private sector.

Some of the problems with estimating plant costs can be attributed to uncertainty surrounding the technology. An incomplete understanding of heat and material balances, scale-up, and difficulties with solids processing are common technical problems encountered in pioneering process plants. Technical uncertainty, however, is only one explanation for poor estimating. Incomplete plant and project definition, bad weather, strikes, labor and material shortages, and regulatory changes can also contribute to cost overruns.

Inaccurate estimates are particularly troublesome for several reasons. Most firms like to determine the means of financing the plant before the project is initiated. Poor cost estimates generally preclude firms from arranging a sufficient amount of financing. Given the poor track record of cost estimators, most companies have increased the percentage of plant cost set aside as contingency costs. This practice is only a temporary solution since improvements in cost estimation and larger contingency budgets could lead to cost overestimation.

The high cost of a commercial scale DCL plant means that even slight inaccuracies in cost estimation can amount to millions of dollars. Fig. 7.9. illustrates the amount of cost overestimation for a sample of large, pioneering process plants. There is every reason to believe that pioneering DCL plants would follow the same pattern.

Figure 7.9.
Cost Growth in Pioneer Energy Process Plants: The Problem

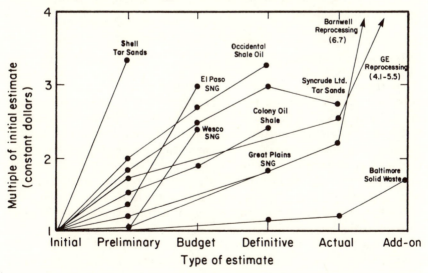

Source: Hess, R. W., et al., *An Analysis of the Cost, Schedule, and Performance of the Baseline SCR-1 Commercial Demonstration Plant,* The Rand Publication Series, Santa Monica, CA (1983), p. 11.

Plant Performance

In addition to a firm's desire to estimate plant costs accurately, companies are equally concerned about producing a product on an efficient and consistent basis. Again, pioneering process plants historically have suffered from poor performance in the first thirty-six months after start-up.[18] In fact, the Rand Corporation found in a survey of over fifty pioneering process plants that less than half of the plants achieved or exceeded a performance level of 90 percent.[19]

Economically, poor plant performance is devastating. A continuous revenue stream is necessary to recover the large initial capital outlays. And given the time value of money, forgone revenue in the earlier stages of plant operation is much more valuable than lower performance at the end of the plant's expected life. One of the experts interviewed for this analysis pointed to high initial capital costs as a major impediment to DCL development: "Capitalization costs alone make up 60% of the selling price of products. There is a need for a chipping away process to reduce costs."

One factor that is uniformly underestimated by owners and operators of pioneering process plants is the time and money required to start up the plant.[20] This is important from a performance perspective since a plant is not considered operational until it meets a certain level of performance. In the same study of forty pioneering process plants, Rand found that most companies never budgeted, or significantly under-budgeted, for start-up costs. Furthermore, less than one third of the plants started up within the planned time frame.

Return on Investment

There must be some incentive for industry to invest in DCL. One approach used by industry is to evaluate their ROI. A successful commercial scale plant would most likely operate at a deficit for several years until conventional oil out-priced the synthetic fuel. In order to make a prudent investment decision, the firm would have to know two things: (1) how long before the product would be able to compete on the market; and (2) the margin of profitability once the product started to compete. For the project to provide a satisfactory ROI, significant profits would have to be realized in later stages of the project to offset the large costs in earlier stages.

One explanation for the dearth of commercial DCL plants in the United States is the inability of firms to show even marginal returns on investment given the prevailing economic conditions. Financial incentives provided by the federal government have been offered over the years in an attempt to encourage private sector involvement in DCL. These government incentives will be discussed in detail below.

Another explanation for the small number of investors in commercial DCL is that the factors discussed above can work independently of each other. In other words, even if a DCL plant is expected to provide a substantial return on the investment, potential cost overruns or poor performance could make the investment unattractive.

PATENTS AS INDICATOR AND PROBLEM IN DCL DEVELOPMENT

The patents registered for DCL give a useful if not precise indicator of activity but, at the same time, they have sometimes posed problems in DCL development. This section examines patterns of patenting but first considers how the patent process has sometimes served as a barrier to DCL development.

Patents as Barrier

The theory behind patents is that they will serve as a legal barrier protecting the pecuniary interests of developers of a technology against those who would seek to draw upon the economic benefits of a technology without having contributed to its development. In practice, however, patents have sometimes served not as a protective barrier but just as a barrier.

In the early history of DCL policy, the federal government held all patent rights to coal liquefaction projects it supported. The theory—a theory upon which most government R&D policy was premised at the time—was that R&D supported by tax dollars should be in the public domain and equally available to all. In practical terms, technology available to all often turns out to be of interest to none. As the policy toward licensing and patenting began to change in the 1960s, the primary property rights-based obstacles to DCL development were diminished with changes in government policy concerning patents for technology flowing from government-sponsored R&D. However, patents still are not the economic wall of protection that some developers hope for. In the first place, patent policy, especially for DOE-sponsored programs, is still not clear-cut and may vary considerably from one DOE regional office to another. Also, licensing agreements still are negotiated in a somewhat ad hoc fashion and often only after protracted deliberations.

At this point in time, however, patent difficulties pose a relatively minor obstacle to DCL development. They are of considerable use as a reflection of DCL activity and, indirectly, productivity.

Patents as Indicator of DCL Development

Fig. 7.10 depicts number of DCL patents, of both U.S. and foreign origin, in the period 1973–1986. For U.S. patents, the curve's incline is steepest in the period 1975–1978, coincident with peak years of synfuels funding. The infusion of synfuels funding seems to have kept patents high, even as funds began to disappear, probably as a lag effect. Notably, the curve for patents of foreign origin (subject to different exogenous variables than U.S. patents) is much smoother. Fig. 7.11 provides information about not only number of patents but also the number produced by the top five and top ten producers, indicating the level of patent concentration. Until patents tumbled in 1986 to a fraction of earlier years, the concentration levels were relatively stable.

For present purposes, a particularly interesting indicator is the number of patents by sector—university, government, industry, other, and U.S. patents abroad (see Fig. 7.10). During the entire period, and as expected, industry has been the leader in patent production, generally responsible for at least 75 percent of the patents produced. Significantly, there seems little prospect that the declines exhibited in industry patents during the past few years will be compensated for by a growth in other sectors' patenting.

Figure 7.10.
Number of Patents Produced by Sector

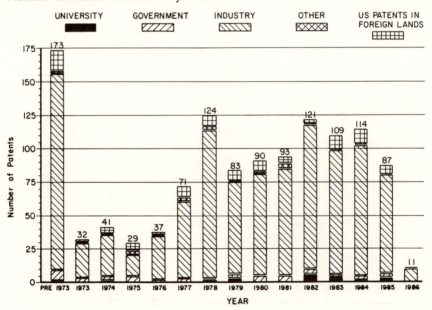

Figure 7.11.
U.S. Patents: Number Produced by the Top Five and Top Ten Producers

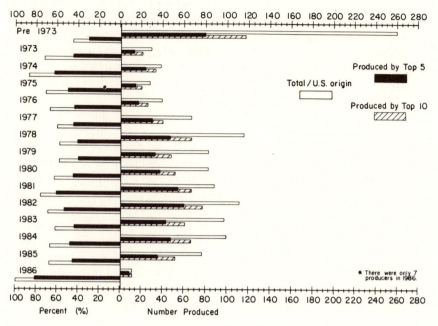

GOVERNMENT SUBSIDIES

Government economic incentives for DCL development can be classified into three broad categories: indirect support through tax policies and trade policies; direct incentive support through loans, loan guarantees, purchase agreements, and price guarantees; and direct monetary support through direct financing of projects and government-owned contractor–operator arrangements.

Tax Policies

The federal government has provided a variety of tax incentives in the past few decades, most not particular to energy development firms. There is some debate as to how useful these incentives have been. Some analysts have argued that oil and gas tax laws have actually worked against the development of DCL.

While it is hard to quantify the exact benefits of these indirect tax and trade policies on DCL, their overall utility should not be underestimated. The adoption of Section 174 of the IRS Code in 1954 was the first of several modern codifications of tax laws pertaining to R&D expenditures of firms. This provision permits businesses to deduct fully research expenditures—but not development—in the year incurred. There is also the option to capitalize research expenditures and amortize them over a period of not less than five years, beginning with the month in which benefits are first realized. By assumption, these benefits occur in the month in which the product or process gained from the research actually produces income, a consideration not as yet relevant to DCL research. This deferral option was intended to benefit the small, newer firms who had little taxable income during their early years.

The IRS made clear that the expending option was limited to direct research expenditures and was not applicable to expenditures on capital assets necessary for the conduct of research and development activities. However, the costs of such depreciable assets as machinery, equipment, and facilities is partly recovered through depreciation allowances that apply for investments in any depreciable property.

While the immediate expensing of research expenditures is viewed generally as an important tax incentive, Kaplan argues that Section 174 is really more an administrative convenience than an incentive. According to Kaplan, "If Congress had truly wanted to supply a tax incentive for R&D, it could have allowed an immediate writeoff for investment in tangible R&D assets [building, machinery, and equipment]."[21] Such an approach would, of course, have proven a much stronger incentive for DCL development.

The most significant recent change in tax treatment of R&D came as a result of the passage of the Economic Recovery Tax Act of 1981 (ERTA). Among the major provisions of ERTA: (1) faster depreciation of R&D assets; (2) two-year suspension of Treasury Regulation 1.861-8 (requiring U.S. multinationals to allocate some of their domestic R&D expenditures against income from foreign sources—an important respite for the oil companies); (3) a tax credit for R&D expenditures.

The tax credit is of particular interest. The credit provided under ERTA, and later extended after its initial lapse period, is 25 percent of the excess of the taxpayer's research for the taxable year over the average of the taxpayer's yearly research expenditure during the base period. The base period is generally defined to be the three years immediately preceding the taxable year for which the credit is claimed. Several limitations are worth noting. In the first place, the requirement for "carrying on a trade or business" means that expenses incurred in connection with trade or business but not pertaining to the development of potentially marketable goods and services fail to qualify. Further, and more important for DCL developers, the credit does not apply to research expenditures paid or incurred prior to commencing a trade or business.

The effects of the ERTA tax credit have been much debated. However, it seems likely that the direct impact on DCL development has been modest because the major expenditures—plant and prototype expenditures—would not be eligible. However, the tax credit should not be considered apart from the accelerated cost recovery provisions provided in ERTA (and later amended in the Tax Equity and Fiscal Responsibility Act of 1982). This legislation provides firms with an incentive to invest in capital equipment by classifying investments into a three-year life or a five-year life. An investment tax credit of 6 percent applies to the three-year property (chiefly vehicles and research equipment) and a 10 percent credit applies to the five-year property (almost all other business equipment and facilities). This initiative is, in a sense, at odds with the tax credit for R&D, owing to the fact that a firm has at least two sources for acquiring new technologies. These sources are crudely dichotomized as being an internal source (i.e., technology generated from in-house R&D), or an external source (technologies embodied in capital equipment and purchases of the firm).[22]

The influence of tax incentives on DCL investments seems modest at best. The major costs—plant and equipment investment—have only recently been recoverable to any considerable extent and, even then, at no more attractive rate than for other non-research relevant plant and equipment recovery. In the scheme of things, the savings resulting from existing tax incentives should not, under most circumstances, be at a sufficiently critical level to have any more than a marginal influence on DCL investment decisions.

Direct Incentive Programs

Direct incentive programs became a popular means of encouraging investment in DCL during the late 1970s and through the 1980s. Most of these incentives were included in the Energy Security Act of 1980, which created the SFC to administer these programs. Some of these programs include:

- Loans and Loan Guarantees: These programs make capital, in large amounts, available at a reasonable interest rate to investors. These government-backed loans are provided to compensate for the reluctance of private lenders to risk capital on pioneering, first-of-a-kind technologies.

- Purchase Agreements: These agreements, generally between the owners of the plant and the government, ensure a market for the synthetic fuels. The government will purchase all or part of the products from the plant at the prevailing market price of the fuel. In certain cases, the purchase price of the fuel will be increased to further encourage investment.

- Price Guarantees: If the market price of petroleum or gas dips below the price of the synthetic fuel, these agreements reimburse the DCL plant owners with the differential.

As an economic instrument, these programs have been a failure. In any attempt to shift more of the risk back to the private sector, these policies have been unable to tilt the economic equation in favor of investment. There are several reasons why these programs have been ineffective. First, and primarily, they have not improved the basic economics of the processes and are viewed by many as creative financing mechanisms. Until the economics of the processes are improved, these incentive programs will be marginally effective. Second, the law that swept in these incentives, many financial analysts fear, could be swept out by another piece of legislation. The Energy Security Act is a particularly good example of this problem.

CONCLUSIONS FROM ECONOMIC MODEL

The conclusions from the economic model do not spring forth quite so easily as one might assume. If there is any central lesson, it is to be wary of deceptively simple economic explanations, to wit:

1. Competitiveness is a moving target. The simple explanation that DCL has not been competitive is cogent but can mislead. First, competitiveness or noncompetitiveness has never been unequivocally demonstrated because a full-scale plant has not been built in the United States. Second, considerations of competitiveness based solely on market variables and distinct from the range of government incentives and extractions is essentially meaningless. In a mixed economy, no set of major economic transactions proceeds in an entirely free market environment, and thus the notion of competitiveness shifts not just with the price of oil (itself an exceptional element for volatility) but also with changes in government incentives and financial extraction policies. The result is that even if the price of oil were entirely stable, the competitiveness of DCL would not be simple to gauge. In sum, the best estimates are that DCL is not currently competitive and that it has not been in the past; however, it is extremely difficult to understand just how much technical efficiency and economic progress are required for competitiveness because the environment changes too rapidly for valid forecasts.

2. Investment calculation for DCL is typically a shell game. The usual investment rules go out the window in the firm's DCL investment calculations. Such a seemingly simple issue as calculating an internal rate of return becomes intolerably complex because of (1) market/public policy interaction effects; (2) novelty (no existing commercial scale activity in the United States); (3) the role of oil not only as a pricing benchmark but also as a production input. No better evidence of the limited validity of investment calculations is needed than examination of government agencies' and firms' calculations of ROI for H-Coal.

3. The economic status of the coal and oil industries have great impact

on DCL investment and policy incentives interact dynamically with industry change. Upon reflection this conclusion seems patent. However, if one takes that conclusion as valid, it puts yet another major hitch in planning DCL development. If industry-level variables are a prime determinant of DCL development, then internal industry factors add a considerable complication. DCL development that is contingent on interest rates, economic growth rates, and inflation is problematic. But if DCL development is to be dependent on the vagaries of business strategy decisions about acquisition, accumulation, and leveraging of debt, and dividend pay-outs, then it becomes another tool for financial maneuvering rather than being evaluated on the basis of its productivity. Relatedly, synfuels policies cannot simultaneously be "welfare" for the developing industry and be critically dependent on the health of the industry for their success.

4. Policies for DCL development have assumed that industry could ultimately be expected to proceed independently once risk has been mitigated. But uncertainty is as much the hindrance as risk. Clearly DCL development is a risky proposition. At different points in time, in different ways, and in different degrees, the federal government has been willing to take steps—loan guarantees, direct grants, and contracts—to help reduce the risk. The central point, however, is that government policies, in all their fluctuations, have done little to reduce uncertainty and may have actually increased it. By not having stable policies for support of DCL and deflection of risk, investment calculations—already highly risky because of the volatility of the price of oil—become even more fraught with uncertainty by not being amenable to reasonably plausible assumptions about the intermediate- to long-range policy of government concerning DCL. As a result, major investment in DCL is not terribly attractive, even with extremely lucrative government incentives, particularly if the incentives are short-lived and not easily predicted.

8 —————— A PUBLIC POLICY-DRIVEN PERSPECTIVE ON DIRECT COAL LIQUEFACTION

One of the possible explanations for the development history of DCL is built around the assumption that public policy has been the guiding force affecting the future of the technology. What this means is that for the purposes of explanation we will assume that the policy process, with all of its inherent decision criteria, political realities, and budgetary characteristics, is the dominant factor in determining the development path of DCL.

In this model we assume that the technology development process is driven by the political economy and not the market economy. As such, the driving force behind the the development of DCL technologies is not related to the market factors of supply and demand in the classical sense. Built around this assumption are the following factors.

1. Demand for DCL technology is a function of perceived political demand for policy action related to oil supply and price fluctuations and not on market demand for replacement fuels.

2. Demand for policy action related to new technology development in the area of DCL is a function of perceived system-level political threats. The political system is threatened by a supply interruption or potential supply shortfall and the policy response is to respond with a series of direct solutions to that real or perceived problem.

3. Demand for the development of DCL technologies is a function of the classic twentieth-century political response to problems of all types. These responses usually include a technological fix and involve large-scale funding.

4. Financing of the technology development process is highly incremental and involves annual political review.

5. Project selection and program funding levels are determined within the political process, and as such, scientific and technical information is of limited utility as a means of influencing final decisions.

6. The market economics of a given technology are not a primary decision criterion in technology development decision making. Important criteria within this model include:

   • speed with which the technological fix can be built as a means of visibly indicating that the policy issue is being addressed;

   • the geopolitical allocation of the potential benefits of the potential program;

   • the political interactions between members of Congress;

   • the politics between the Congress and the administration;

   • the level and type of public opinion regarding the policy issue being evaluated;

   • the placement and position of the issue on the national agenda;

   • the perceived level of external threat to which the technological solution might be a viable response.

The model suggested above indicates that it is the nature of the policy process in the context of the technology issue at hand that defines the way in which the technology will develop. To illustrate this point, the public policy related to DCL development will be reviewed for the period 1943–present. In this context we will attempt to explain DCL developments as they have occurred.

THE POLICY HISTORY

Since 1943 the U.S. government has launched several efforts to stimulate the development of synthetic fuels. In each of these efforts the political and policy factors that have influenced the technology development process have varied. Thus they merit brief review at this time. Each of the periods presented in the introduction are again reviewed below.

Early U.S. Experimentation Period (1943–1957)

During World War II the United States became aware of the fact that the Nazi regime had expanded on its ability to produce synthetic fuels to the extent that it had become a major factor in the fueling of the German air force. This technological threat, as well as the perception that fuel supplies could possibly become scarce, led the government to launch an effort to develop synthetic fuels, including the DCL option. A brief review of the policy environment in this period is detailed below.

In response to the perceived technological threat of German synthetic fuel production, the U.S. Congress initiated in 1943 a program to construct and operate demonstration plants capable of producing synthetic liquid fuels from coal and oil shales. The need for these demonstration plants was justified on the basis that they could serve as the means for the development of a commercial synthetic fuels industry. The specific need for the demonstration program was justified based on:

- the need for stable low cost fuel for the war effort;
- the need to provide stable and large scale employment opportunities after the war;
- technological power and prestige in the world;
- recognition that the petroleum supplies are finite and the belief that there were only about 50 years of supply remaining;
- the fact that private industry had no incentive to conduct large-scale demonstrations without government support.

In this policy period it was assumed that the technology was ready for development and that what was needed was the construction of several demonstration plants. There seemed to be general agreement among the various interest groups that a program was needed at the time. Included in the support group were the National Coal Association and various federal agencies, including the War Department. The only noticeable group opposing the program at the time of the Congressional initiative was the oil industry. In hearings before the Congress, representatives from the Standard Oil Company presented evidence that the development of synthetic liquids from coal would require unrealistic levels of capital and equipment when compared with existing refining technology.[1] It is important to note that the key actors in pushing this program were the senior officials from the War Department. Their primary justification was the rate of petroleum resource depletion.

In FY 1945, funds were appropriated to initiate the design and conceptualization work associated with the potential start-up of the program. In addition, Congress authorized a large-scale demonstration program, still as a means of addressing what many officials perceived as an impending petroleum shortage. In this sense this first major effort at demonstrating DCL technology was a political response to a potential crisis—the crisis was a fuel shortage, more than likely after the war and more than likely in the commercial and industrial sector. This shortage, because of the nature of the war effort, was not generally known to the public. Thus the push for synthetic fuels development, particularly DCL, was generated within the highest levels of the federal government.

Between FY 1946 and FY 1948 the debate as to whether or not to actually build demonstration plants began to develop. The debate centered on the use of a wartime authorization to continue to develop a new program. There were many, particularly in the House, who felt that the government should learn how to build the plants but refrain from building demonstration facilities. The decision to proceed with a limited number of demonstration plants eventually prevailed and plant development efforts were begun.

By 1950, the government's synthetic fuel program had been running for two fiscal years and was operating at $10 million/year. As early as this date the processes associated with converting shale to oil already seemed to be the farthest along. On the political front the justification for continued development of DCL began to be more directly linked to the geopolitics of coal. As a result, substantial bickering between the House and the Senate became common as to the size, scope, and location of various program facilities.

In April 1951, Congress held a series of hearings on the status of the synthetic fuel and DCL demonstration effort. In this debate the argument on which the initial synfuels effort was based—the petroleum supply problem—began to be discredited. This was at least partially the result of the fact that the anticipated oil supply interruption never occurred. The major Middle Eastern oil fields were beginning to open around this time, and large new U.S. oil fields were beginning to be developed. In short, the political impetus for the project was beginning to disappear. Nonetheless the Bureau of Mines was moving ahead to implement the program at a number of sites. In 1952 these sites included: Bruceton, Pennsylvania; Morgantown, West Virginia; Louisiana, Missouri; Laramie, Wyoming; Rifle, Colorado; and Gorgas, Alabama.

In FY 1953, with the advent of the Eisenhower administration and the first movement of industry into a significant opposition role against the program, the nature of the political contest changed. For the first time there was substantial conflict regarding the role of the government in this overall effort as well as conflict surrounding the specific demonstration projects being pursued by the government. It is perceived by some that industry began to feel threatened by the possibility that the government would develop generic processes capable of developing a politically viable, if not economically viable, alternative to petroleum.[2] Industry, with the change in administrations, therefore felt it had the means to oppose the program. In addition, the significant ideological changes that began to occur in the Congress around this time were indicative of a new perception of the role of the government in program development type activities.

With waning political support and with the initial authorization scheduled to expire in 1955, the government's synthetic fuel efforts and DCL program initiatives were terminated in 1955. In the period 1944–1955 the government had established several demonstration facilities, operated a major demonstration project for the production of liquid fuels from coal, and evaluated several other processes for the possible direct conversion of coal. In essence the government, largely operating on its own, demonstrated that the DCL technology developed by the Germans was viable in the United States.

The political demand for the program was largely based on the perception that oil was a resource that would prove finite in the foreseeable future and that the United States had to be a technological leader in all important areas of technology. When the political demand for a replacement fuel for petroleum waned in the early 1950s, combined with the movement from a liberal to a conservative government in 1953, the political demand function for DCL was reduced to a level below that necessary for sustaining the program.

After 1955 the U.S. Bureau of Mines, as the lead government agency, continued to attempt to acquire funding for DCL development work but was unsuccessful. Final reports were prepared, and the technology was placed on the shelf for use in periods of increased political demand for oil replacement.

Office of Coal Research Era: The Institutionalization of Coal Research (1961–1973)

Coal had always been a politically important topic in the halls of Congress and in Washington. It was an industry linked to the well-being of the entire nation and one that was deemed to be an important basic industry for the American industrial enterprise. As such it was an industry that was highly visible from a political perspective. Associated with the industry had always been an undercurrent of labor problems. In the background, beyond the labor problems, had always been the awareness of a range of social problems associated with the coal industry, particularly in the Appalachian region.

It is not surprising then that as a part of the 1960 presidential campaign the social problems associated with Appalachia became a national agenda item for the Democrats. Within this context several solutions to the problem of poverty in Appalachia were discussed. With the election of a Democratic administration in 1960 several new programs were initiated. In addition to the Appalachian Regional Commission (developed in the early 1960s), with its economic development role, the administration also permitted the development of a small-scale Office of Coal Research. Created in 1961, the Office of Coal Research (OCR) was developed as a small research enterprise designed to stimulate the expanded use of coal. The political problem facing the Congress at the time was that in addition to the continuing social problems associated with the

Table 8.1.
Funding Trends for Office of Coal
Research: 1961–1974

Year	Amount Appropriated
1961	$ 1,000,000
1962	1,000,000
1963	3,450,000
1964	5,750,000
1965	6,836,000
1966	7,220,000
1967	8,220,000
1968	10,980,000
1969	13,700,000
1970	15,300,000
1971	17,160,000
1972	30,650,000
1973	43,490,000
1974	123,400,000

Appalachian region, the coal industry itself, the region's only significant industry, was in decline. Demand for coal in the United States was at its lowest point in decades and it was anticipated that with cheap petroleum supplies being made available, demand would continue to fall.

With a new political demand for coal research, now based on the social needs of a particular region, a second push for the demonstration of DCL technologies slowly began to emerge. As shown in Table 8.1, funding for OCR began quite modestly and grew by increments between 1963 and 1971. After 1971 funding began to increase in larger increments, and finally in 1973/74, with recognition of the emerging oil crisis, funding increased from $43 million to $123 million.

An analysis of the development of the OCR as an agency reveals that it was highly politicized in the sense that particular members of Congress (those from areas most likely to benefit from development of synthetic fuel technologies) were closely involved in the agency's development. In addition, a coalition representing the coal interests in the West (i.e., versus the coal interests in the East) developed as a means of expanding the total scope of the program.

Several characteristics of the period reflect the character of political environment:

• The major focus of project selection discussions in Congress was on project location. Project selection criteria focused on the distribution of projects into those areas with congressional representation on key committees. Of course, there already existed a natural tendency to place members from the large coal states on the committees with jurisdiction over the OCR program.

• OCR, because of its complicated coalition of supporters from the various coal regions, was always having to base its project selection on the relative political criteria of resource distribution among the projects supported by the various members.

• Within OCR the practice of reprogramming was frequently used as a means of "finding" money for favored projects. This was particularly true for those projects affiliated with the state of West Virginia and Senator Robert Byrd. Senator Byrd was clearly the dominant political force behind OCR and appeared to be the key political broker in developing the OCR budget.

• The budget pattern was that the House would always lower the president's budget request and the Senate would increase it. Supplemental appropriations were common as many of the projects required additional funding for a range of reasons in a specific state.

• Projects all seem to have been sold on the basis that they could be demonstrated in the relatively short term. Following initial funding, projects were sustained well beyond their initial projections. Again, because projects were directed more toward economic development than research and development, the typical justification used for additional project funding was that it would lead to the eventual revitalization of the coal industry in particular regions. In this sense the DCL program of the 1960s and early 1970s was a technological fix to a series of social problems in various regions. This was similar to the government's approach to the TVA and to the major water projects common in the South and West.

• The emphasis of congressional review and oversight of these programs was on the ability of these efforts to create jobs in individual states.

• Attainment of project technical goals appears to have been of secondary interest to congressional reviewers. In fact none of the major DCL projects initiated by OCR in this period were ever on budget or on time.

Beginning in 1974, the overall level of funding and the scope of the program began to increase beyond the historical incremental levels. These increases were associated with the expansion of the overall synthetic fuels development effort as well as the movement into larger scale demonstration projects. Interestingly, DCL funding between FY 1972 and FY 1973 declined in real dollars. In FY 1974, however, with the recognition that oil supply interruptions were eminent, the DCL program budget was increased by a factor of three. Again, as the threat of supply shortfalls became evident, the political economy demanded government action directed toward the replacement of liquid fuels, and liquid fuels could best be produced by the direct conversion of coal to synthetic oil (or at least it was so thought by policymakers at the time).

The result of this major push in FY 1974 was the rapid movement toward the demonstration of a number of DCL options in a short period of time. The emphasis again was on demonstration and not on R&D, as it was perceived by most that the technology was already viable for demonstration type activities.

The Oil Crisis Period (1974–1982)

After years of relatively small-scale program activity, most of which seemed to have the character of WPA projects, the government found itself in an environment of intense political pressure for immediate response to a rapid increase in the price of petroleum. This political demand was manifested in complaints about gas lines and fuel shortages and in no uncertain terms resulted in a crisis type mentality in the government. This intense political demand resulted in the tenfold expansion of DCL demonstration efforts, the rapid expansion of the government's staff in this program area, and the rapid reorganization of the national energy research bureaucracy, first into the consolidated Energy Research and Development Administration (1975) and later into the cabinet level Department of Energy (1977). These political responses were implemented with considerable difficulty.

From 1975 until roughly 1981, the government responded to the political demand for action against the threat of oil supply and price fluctuations with the decision to launch a major, fast-track demonstration program in DCL and other synthetic fuel options. The policy plan was again based on the premise that DCL was a viable technology lacking only the funding necessary for success. Projects were again sold on the basis of short turnaround time for successful demonstration and ultimate commercialization. Also at this time the political distributional character of the program, so prevalent in the previous period, began to occur in the development of the demonstration projects.

Throughout this period the program gained momentum as political demand for action increased following the second oil shock of 1979. The resulting program expanded to include a research program, a major demonstration program, and in 1980 the initiation of a comprehensive, massive program of loans and market guarantees for the commercialization of various synthetic fuel options including, but certainly not limited to, DCL. The ultimate goal of this large program effort was the production of industrial quantities of synthetic fuels. It was perceived at the time that as a part of a rational national energy policy, synthetic fuels would be moved toward commercial production scale regardless of the fact that the process economics might not be competitive with natural fuels.

During this period the government began the process of letting large comprehensive development contracts to a number of competing industries with DCL process configurations. These contracts were intended to provide the government with a number of competing process configurations. These competing configurations would be developed as a means of addressing the various types of coals in the United States. More importantly from a policy perspective was the fact that the demonstration projects needed to be located in various regions of the United States as a means of gaining support. While the siting of plants solely according to the political desires of the members of Congress from a given state, as was the case with the Cresap Project, was less common in this period, geopolitics remained an important project siting variable.

An important distinction between this period and other development thrusts was that, because of the scale involved in these demonstration projects and the ultimate scale and technical risk associated with the commercialization of any process, industry had to be a major financial partner in the process development efforts. As such this would imply that the involvement of industry in the political process would subsequently increase. Even though it is relatively clear that industry did not fully support the development of a commercial synthetic fuels technology, it is also clear that in the early days of the energy crisis (1974–1979) there was little room for any U.S.-based energy company not to participate in the technology development competition. This is particularly true because of the fact that the government was going to take most of the risk and put up most of the demonstration capital. U.S. energy companies found themselves in a policy situation where they were uncertain as to whether the outcome might include mandatory production of synthetic fuels. Given this kind of possibility the incentives were strong for energy companies to at least be a joint sponsor in a particular technology area.

The H-coal process and several other projects were placed on a fast-track development time frame. Rapid funding and staffing increases resulted in the development of new technology developments in the various processes and in the determination of the viability of these various projects as the means by which to meet the synthetic fuel goals.

In 1981 the several DCL processes that were moving toward demonstration and (as it was then planned) toward commercialization before 1985, were viewed as expensive options in the synthetic fuel production game. From a policy perspective, then, these processes, except for their attractiveness in the Eastern coal states, were viewed as less-than-viable options for ultimate selection as demonstration projects, as compared with other projects. As such, DCL as an option began to lose some of its political support compared with other synthetic fuel options. With the loss of political support the mechanism developed for the commercialization of various synthetic fuel technologies; the Synthetic Fuels Corporation, with its associated market and loan guarantees, began to look upon the various DCL options as too risky for even its investment. At the time there were several competing technologies in the political economy. Given that a dominant concern within the political economy was time-to-solution, it began to become obvious that DCL, which lagged by several years, could not be developed in the same time frame. The result of this was that by as early as 1982 DCL processes were once again beginning to lose support.

Technology on Hold (1982–Present)

If events in 1980 were optimistic for synthetic fuels and DCL, then by 1982 the exact opposite was true. Once again, as was the case with the demise of the program in the 1950s, the development of DCL as a synthetic fuels technology option was threatened by the onset of a con-servative, free-market-oriented administration and the apparent diminu-tion of the external oil supply threat. These two factors together greatly reduced the level of political demand for all synthetic fuels and led to the initiation of the demise of the entire program. In 1982 the condition of the development of the synthetic fuel industry was summarized by gov-ernment officials and industry executives as follows[3]:

- The combination of soft oil prices, high interest rates, and the general eco-nomic recession convinced many potential investors that 1982 and beyond was not the time to invest in the industry.
- Evidence began to surface that the costs of scaling-up to full commercial-size plants were higher and involved more risks than had previously been con-sidered.
- Commercial lending institutions, a critical element in the eventual develop-ment of DCL or any other synthetic fuel technology, were at the time unwilling to lend money without at least federal loan guarantees.

Each of these factors indicate that by as early as 1982 not only had the political demand for DCL diminished but so had the potential political support for further policy development by the future synthetic fuel in-dustry as well as the finance industry, which would be an integral part of the overall industrial development effort. The result was that there was insufficient political demand to sustain and ultimately implement the truly massive effort required to develop a commercial synthetic fuels industry. Given that DCL within this context was already not at the top of the development list, it was clear, at least from a political expediency perspective, that as a technology development option it was again enter-ing a period where the technology development process would be terminated.

Partially as an analog of the reduced political demand for a tech-nological fix to the waning energy problem, the advent of the Reagan administration in 1981 brought about an ideological change regarding what the role of the government should be in the area of technology development. By 1982 the Reagan administration began an effort to limit the powers of and eventually abolish the Synthetic Fuels Corporation (SFC). The specific manifestations of this policy shift that were apparent at the time included[4]:

- The supply-side ideological assumptions of the Reagan administration, plus severe budget pressures within the policy process, are seen as being inconsistent with large-scale government support for any synthetic fuel program. With the decrease in political demand for action it became increasingly difficult to justify a major federal program in technology development. In its stead the Reagan administration developed policy responses that at least from the perspective of 1982 appeared to be more in tune with the perceived political demand for quick action. These policy options included accelerating the filling of the national strategic petroleum reserve and implementation of a rapid deployment force to respond to threats to the petroleum supplies in the Middle East.

- Because of the lack of political demand for its services and the associated lack of political support for development of a comprehensive synthetic fuels industry, the SFC began to adopt a far slower and more cautious approach. The result of this was that the SFC began to come under attack from opponents and supporters alike for being inefficient and unable to move projects forward. Initial project selections by the SFC favored small projects and involved focusing on those technologies from various parts of the country.

- The lack of clear environmental policy for the first time began to impede the ability of major projects to proceed. One interviewee commented on the mixed and unclear signals and their implications for DCL development: "The 1960s were a period of tough market. A good deal of competition and little room to cut costs. The utilities developed during this period a coal cost model that would forecast a cost per million Btu's at a particular boiler based on mine-mouth coal costs, transportation costs, cleaning costs, etc. Utilities were not willing to pay premium prices for cleaner coal if they could meet constraints they were under at that time with a cheaper, dirtier coal."

- About this time were seen the beginning movements toward termination, through budget reductions, staff reductions, and program rescissions, of all synthetic fuel technology demonstration programs.

Each of these points contributed to the systematic dismantling of the synthetic fuels program and with it the DCL R&D effort. In fact DCL projects were already in trouble in the sense that the political maneuvering of the SFC to adapt to a changing political climate limited the type, number, and scope of projects to be undertaken by the SFC. This limitation essentially eliminated the potential for commercial development of DCL processes by as early as 1984. Until this point it had remained possible that the demonstration developments in DCL might have the opportunity for continued development and commercialization.

Between 1982 and 1986 the national policy for the development of technology and the subsequent production of synthetic fuels was dismantled. With the movement of R&D budgets back to funding levels associated with the 1950–1960 period and with the demise of the SFC and all of its charter in 1986, the latest of the three phases in the development of a synthetic fuels technology base in the United States since 1944 ended without having attained its goal.

CONCLUSIONS FROM ANALYSIS OF THE POLICY MODEL

After having presented on overview of policy developments pertaining to DCL development and systematically providing answers to the questions driving the "interviewing the data" methodology (see Appendix to this chapter), it is useful to distill conclusions about the influence of political and policy process factors on DCL. Arguably, many of the conclusions appropriate to DCL provide at least the germ of lessons for technology development/public policy interactions of a variety of types in diverse settings. To that end, the ensuing conclusions are broad-based and may be thought of as preliminary hypotheses for a burgeoning theory of technology development (other components of this "pre-theory" are suggested as alternative models, economic and technological).

While a major purpose here is to provide valid explanations and perhaps even the first blush of theory, the conclusions presented seem to us to have direct practical implications for the design and assessment of public policy. The practical implications are discussed in conjunction with each of the major conclusions.

1. Flaws in DCL development are attributable in large measure to the discontinuities in public policy. The course of public policy rarely runs smooth. Indeed, it is naïve to expect that public policies will unfold in predictable ways that are entirely salutary for the public interest or for the professed goals of legislation and policy actors. But the case of DCL is special. A number of factors seem to have conspired against the even and unfettered development of DCL. Taken separately, any one of these factors would have limited the prospects of "rational" policy development. Taken together, they virtually assured that DCL development would proceed in fits and jerks and to no good end.

Political succession at the highest level—presidential administration and Congressional composition—have made an indelible mark on DCL development. To some extent presidents are captives of events. But each president has distinct policy preferences—sometimes well-developed ideological postures—that explain much about their respective administration's approach to governance as well as particular policy preferences. Presidents set agendas. More to the point, this is as it should be. As the only official elected by all the voters, it has come to be expected that the president will serve as chief legislator and that that periods of presidential succession will serve as an impetus to change. But while there are many desirable features of "the new broom sweeping clean," not all public policies are equally adaptable to quick shifts in levels of financial and political commitment. Of all categories of public policy, large-scale R&D based technology development projects may be the most adversely affected by dramatic change. Indeed, "up cycles" are sometimes nearly as harmful as "down cycles." During up cycles of funding and policy support the R&D infrastructure in industry and government is often unprepared for the latest big push and, as a result, has a difficult time using resources wisely and with optimal results. By the same token, the rapid decline in support results in all manner of dislocation—personnel, project, financial, and, most important, scientific and technical.

As the overview of DCL development indicated, presidential change has been associated with dramatic changes in support for DCL. Clearly, some of this change was correlational—Jimmy Carter supported unprecedented synfuels growth but he also presided over what was generally perceived as the greatest energy crisis faced by the United States. Nevertheless, presidential "policy philosophies" (for want of a better term) seem to have played a singular role in DCL development. It is not just whether there is a perceived energy crisis; presidents have different ideas about the role of government, particularly vis-à-vis the marketplace. These views often have pervasive influence. Sometimes the changes are more cosmetic than real (for instance, the substitution of tax incentives for grants and payments) but other times they result in fundamental changes in policy agendas.[5] This certainly seems to have been the case with DCL development policies—it makes a difference who is in the White House.

It also makes a difference who is in the Congress. Much of the micro-politics of DCL development is played out in the U.S. Congress and, of course, electoral change takes place twice as often (or two-thirds as often) in Congress as in the presidency. However, congressional change has had a somewhat less pronounced effect (than presidential change) because changes in Congress tend to be buffered by the fact that only a relatively small percentage of Congress changes at any one time. Also, the fact that the leadership, based on seniority, plays a more prominent role, means that there is another built-in force for stability. Still, congressional change can also lead to discontinuities, especially when change results in turnover of key committee chairmen or a change in the majority party. As is discussed below, Congress brings another set of problems (in addition to change) to DCL development.

It is worth noting that the stop-and-go pattern exhibited in public support for DCL is found as well in many of the relevant interest groups concerned with energy policy. A conspicuous example is the American Petroleum Institute (API), which alternated between being the best friend and worst enemy of synfuels in general and DCL in particular. The strange bedfellows cliché describing political mating is perhaps no better exemplified than in the 1980 coalition to stop synfuels support—a coalition composed of, among others, the API and the environmental lobby.

The discontinuity problem, if we may call it that, is not an easy one to remedy. One approach might be to establish an independent agency, presumably less immune to external political influence and less concerned with temporal events, and give the agency authority for disbursing funds to support DCL R&D. This is, of course, exactly the idea behind the Synfuels Corporation, an idea whose time has come—and gone. Another approach, less tried but perhaps also less true, would be to cultivate further involvement of the Department of Defense in DCL. If there is limited support for DCL on the basis of short-term market need or presidential policy initiative, it is reasonable to view DCL and other selected synthetic fuels options in terms of national security. The market is volatile, such that the demand for alternative energy supplies could alter in the relatively short period of a year or two. But a national security-driven demand could occur literally overnight. This seems an eminently reasonable peg upon which to hang the rationale for a critical mass level of continuous and stable support for DCL.

This view was reflected by one of the experts interviewed for this project: "Possibly the filling of the strategic oil reserve would be the way to bring industry back in. When fuel supply becomes a concern again government will need to fund research by private organizations, universities and other institutions. In the meantime, government funds should be set aside to find new ways to upgrade coal, develop new catalysts, and develop an improved knowledge of coal structure."

Another interviewee echoed the importance of DCL for energy security: "Fuel is a strategic material. DCL is a viable option to build fuel reserves. The government should look at DCL as a strategic opportunity."

2. DCL has been victimized by pork-barrel politics. Any public policy that involves large expenditures of money, concentrated in a relatively small geographical region, is a prime candidate for the political pork barrel. When that policy also supports a fundamental basis of a state's or region's economy and when it includes jobs and capital construction projects, political jockeying intensifies even further. The infusion of regional political concerns is not necessarily ignominious. Sometimes the pluralistic processes of congressional backscratching turn out, usually

indirectly, to favor equity concerns. Harlan County, Kentucky, might not compete with Route 128 (in Massachusetts) on most bases, but it might on the basis of the seniority and influence of its congressman. As one of the interviewees for this study noted: "In some states, especially Kentucky and West Virginia, where they have coal and the necessary water and power, the politicians have, of course, pushed for coal liquefaction and all other uses of coal for that matter."

While pork-barrel politics is not always damaging, it is likely to prove a problem for projects having quite specific technical or resource requirements not easily met at a variety of sites. As the evidence in this chapter suggests, plant siting often had a great deal too much to do with the distribution of power in Congress (and in statehouses) and too little to do with the requirements of plants for particular feedstocks, skilled personnel, and so forth. In extreme cases, distributional politics can change the direction of not only specific projects but entire streams of research. The case of the OCR's Cresap project, detailed elsewhere in this report, is an example of such an extreme effect. In this instance the single project was so costly, albeit wrongheaded, that it sapped the modest OCR budget to the breaking point. One explanation of the failure of H-coal to reach the takeoff point is that necessary funds were diverted at a critical time from H-coal to the Cresap project.

As with the discontinuity problem, the difficulties flowing from pork-barrel politics are nearly intractable. To the extent there is a "solution" to an axiomatic principle of politics, it might lie in changing the nexus for decisions about plant and facility siting. Congress will, and often should, have a role in major decisions about facilities, but that role should not be peremptory. There is precedent for blue ribbon panels to be in charge of major equipment and facility siting decisions. The National Institutes for Health routinely make such decisions in this manner. Perhaps such an approach could be extended to at least some of the major siting decisions for DCL plants. Presently, the issue may be moot, but that is all the more reason to move as soon as possible on revising siting procedures—now might be the time of least political resistance.

3. The quick fix is not the answer. Much of DCL development has been part and parcel of the tendency for policymakers to search for the quick fix. Sometimes policies have been quick on the uptake, but rarely has there been a fix.

Policymaking often proceeds according to reactions to perceived crisis. The tendency of policymakers to think of DCL in comparison with a volatile benchmark—the price and availability of oil—accelerates the tendency toward the quick-fix approach to policymaking. The history of DCL policy is one marked more by fear than opportunity. When the national anxiety level, and in turn the political barometer, reach the saturation point, it begins to rain synfuel dollars. By the same token, when the crisis "goes away," synfuel dollars go away. The search for the quick fix is the root of many policy maladies. From one standpoint, it is simply inefficient. If policies and research agendas are formulated hurriedly in response to crisis, then the likelihood of careful expenditure of limited resources is greatly reduced. This is no less true for DCL than for other policy arenas.[6]

The quick-fix problem is, of course, related to the discontinuity problem. But, as framed above, the discontinuity problem is more a matter of policymakers' having diverse agendas and short periods to implement them. The quick-fix problem is less a function of political succession than of reactive policymaking.

The solution to the quick fix is obvious in concept but not easily realized: There is a need for a stable funding base. It is reasonable, or at any rate unavoidable, that levels of support for DCL (and most policy domains related to the national interest) will be subject to swings of the perceived crisis pendulum. However, once an adequate base level of support is developed, additional funds could be deployed to accelerate current R&D efforts rather than to fund multiple new (and sometimes poorly thought out) start-ups.

4. Policymakers for DCL are ensnared in the "overadvocacy trap." There is an unfortunate tendency of policymakers to oversell poorly understood programs with high levels of uncertainty and thus fall into the overadvocacy trap. Officials in federal agencies are among those most often victimized by the overadvocacy trap. This might seem at odds with the popular stereotype of the cautious, risk-averse bureaucrat. But there are good reasons, especially in the case of DCL policy, why claims often fly quickly by actual potential.

One cause of the overselling of DCL policy relates back to the issue of the quick fix. Agency officials recognize that policymaking is driven by reactions to crisis, that policy proceeds in spurts, and that issues ignored yesterday by Congress often turn out to be today's hot ticket. This means that agency officials usually have to be prepared to sell their wares while the selling is good. If an item is on the congressional or presidential agenda, there is no guaranteeing how long it will be there. There are pressures to exploit political anxieties by offering up policy palliatives. Congressmen reacting to crisis are not anxious to hear that a project might come to fruition if it is carefully nurtured for a decade or so. Knowing this, agency officials (and other supporters of DCL development) are likely to tell congressmen what they want to hear—that there is a *deus ex machina* just in sight.

The supposition, often quite reasonable, is that many of the actors will have changed in any case when (and if) the technology is called to account. If this tendency to oversell were only an innocuous part of a highly stylized game of political show and tell, there would be no cause for concern about its possible effects on the development of DCL. But there is some evidence, as discussed in this chapter, that the tendency to overadvocate leads to bad investment decisions, poor estimates of risk, and questionable policy choices. Sometimes the most glamorous project is not the one with the highest marginal return on investment of DCL dollars. A possible current example is biological processing of coal, which to date has generated much excitement but little in the way of hard solutions to DCL development problems.

5. DCL policy has been based on an assumption of government/business cooperation—a dubious assumption. No DCL development project has proceeded to pilot plant development in the absence of government support. Industry initiatives not relying on government funding have been uncommon and small-scale. DCL development has, in each major case, been a joint enterprise with government playing a role ranging from funding conduit to full-scale partner. Significantly, the Synfuels Liquid Fuel Act of 1944, the first major U.S. initiative, could be viewed as the first of several government attempts to create a U.S. synfuels industry. In virtually every case of major DCL development there has been a presumption of government/industry cooperation. In many instances this presumption has been more than the development process could bear.

There are a number of respects in which the needed government/business partnership has been star-crossed. In the first place, one of the major business participants in the synfuels coalition has been ambivalent about the mission of developing a synfuels industry: The petroleum industry, a necessary ingredient to synfuels development, has blown hot and cold on DCL, at times developing major projects, at times opposing development of DCL. The petroleum industry's ambivalence is understandable. At the outset, it was clear that synfuels could be a competitor to their products as easily as an extension of their product line. Any early attempt by industry to form a patent rights pooling mechanism was thwarted by the government as OCR decided that patent rights should be controlled by the government. Government control of patent rights has been a disincentive to industry involvement in virtually every technological realm in which that arrangement has emerged. Another reason for the oil industry's understandable reluctance to jump into the synfuels fray is that synfuel policies have not been evenhanded in their effects on particular industries or even particular businesses.

Synfuels policy has in some instances been "welfare for the coal industry." It is assumed by government that there are positive direct and indirect effects for the health of the coal industry, and synfuels investments are sometimes rationalized not only in terms of energy needs but in terms of industrial support. The petroleum industry has been harangued as often as encouraged by synfuels policymakers. Even at the beginnings of government policy activity (circa 1944–1950), Interior/OCR officials and the petroleum industry found themselves at odds. Early OCR estimates indicated that DCL processes developed by the Germans and technologically verified by early research were economically competitive with the cost of oil (production costs of 11 cents per gallon). The clear implication was that if the plodding petroleum industry would only seize the opportunity, the United States would have another major source of energy. Understandably, the industry disputed the production cost claims and the implications and the clamor intensified.

Two other thorns in the government/business partnership relate to points made above. On balance, the pork-barrel nature of DCL plant and equipment siting decisions has served to undermine the confidence and enthusiam of business. Surely some businesses have been "winners" in the pork-barrel competition, but in the long run decisions governed by the usual rules of distributional politics have the effect of introducing an element of unpredictability into the business decision equation, one that is often enough to preclude interest in DCL development. The discontinuities of political turnover have also affected government/business relations. Different presidents have had different views of the role of government in business and this has led to the kinds of policy inconsistencies of which business decision makers are understandably wary.

A final point is worth noting even though it is difficult to document. Business and government are two distinct cultures or, more accurately, two quite different sets of cultures. Even pro-business administrations such as the Reagan administration tend to be distrusted by business leaders. This culture clash is understandable. For one thing, government, even the Reagan administration, is presumably driven by the need to provide goods and services to meet collective needs of the public. Business is driven by the need to derive private benefits appropriated to some and not to others. This is a simple point and would likely draw few objections. However, public policy often seems to underestimate the extent to which these quite distinct sets of values can come together in beneficial ways. The development of DCL is a useful cautionary note to those too optimistic about bringing together diverse values in pursuit of a set of common goals.

9 ——————— *CONCLUSIONS: THE EFFECTS OF SUPPORT HIATUS ON DIRECT COAL LIQUEFACTION DEVELOPMENT*

The purpose of this concluding chapter is to distill the information provided by each of the perspective chapters—economic, policy, technological, and, generally, historical—and draw broad conclusions. These conclusions represent a synthesis of the various perspectives taken.

A number of assumptions were made about the role of these conclusions in this analysis. First, as mentioned above, it was assumed that the conclusions should have considerable breadth. Each of the preceding chapters presents conclusions, and there is no wish to present merely a summary of the conclusions drawn previously. Yet, at the same time, it is desirable that the conclusions presented here encompass the major points presented in the preceding chapters. Naturally, any synthesis requires subsidiary knowledge. Finally, the focus is on conclusions that have some potential policy relevance. Had the purpose of this analysis been purely historical, the conclusions presented might be somewhat different and might focus a bit more on the role of unique events. But the concern here is to provide conclusions that seem a valid reading of the history of DCL development but, at the same time, have implications for public policy, particularly in the area of large-scale public technology.

There are six principal conclusions presented or, more accurately, five conclusions and one overarching theme. It is perhaps useful to summarize these conclusions before discussing them in more detail.

1. Pioneering technology cannot be assessed as can conventional technologies. Problems in management of plants, in engineering, or in equipment maintenance have been viewed as extraordinary, but in fact they should be expected

and accepted as routine. Assessments of technical efficiency applied to pioneering processes and plants require different standards.

2. DCL is best viewed as government-sheltered high technology development (not industry development). DCL development policy has been premised on government/business partnership and the building up of DCL as market-competitive industry. DCL should be developed whether or not industry is interested and should be rationalized in national security/energy security terms. Short- or intermediate-term competitiveness with the price of petroleum should be a less relevant consideration. Policies should be similar to those used to build the computer industry: overspecification of performance at cost-plus, guaranteed purchase for government stockpiles, procurement-based incentives.

3. DCL represents technological advance but competitive failure; information management should be improved. Currently several DCL technologies have developed to the point that they can be considered commercial. Yet at the same time they are not commercially viable in a market-driven environment. They cannot, and through incremental improvements they will not, overcome the difference of a factor of two in the price of commercial fuel. If DCL is constrained to operate in a market-driven environment, only fundamental new developments will save the concept of liquid fuels derived directly from coal. One key is to use current information more effectively and to encourage cross-fertilization among DCL researchers and others working on separate but potentially relevant problems.

4. Limited resources have been spread too thin: Small technological increments have been spread out over multiple projects. The result is that not enough attention has been given to sustained development of the strongest candidate technologies.

5. Invest in contingency planning. DCL policy has typically been developed in the context of the immediate events: current crisis, current energy availability, current federal budgetary climate. DCL and synfuels generally require longer-range thinking and contingency planning.

Overarching Theme: The hiatus effect. The constant changing of policy and the on-again-off-again nature of support for DCL have undermined development efforts. DCL development requires some long-run, sustained development activity.

Pioneering Processes Cannot Be Assessed Like Conventional Technologies

Throughout the development of DCL two points have been particularly troublesome: (1) it has never been "competitive" with the price of petroleum; (2) pilot plant, demonstration, and maintenance costs have been "excessive." In the following section we consider the problems with the competitiveness criterion; here we suggest that the excessive operational costs have been misinterpreted.

The government experience in developing high technology in synthetic fuels has not paralleled the high technology development role in space or defense. Consider the case of computer technology. Many observers seem to feel that the federal government played a central role in early and intermediate development of computers "overspecification" of quality control and materials standards, by procurement policies guaranteeing sales and, most relevant to the present point, by maintaining expectations appropriate to the state-of-the-science at a given point in development.[1] One might argue that the federal government could afford a more tolerant attitude about the technical efficiency and payoff of computers because of their enormous commercial potential. But this would be an inaccurate interpretation of the early history of government support for computers: Early forecasts implied that the world market for mainframe computers would never exceed an installed base of 500.[2]

In any discussion of DCL it is important to remember that not a single full-scale plant has ever existed in the United States. Nonetheless, evaluation standards for pilot plants have sometimes been almost as demanding as one would expect for a fully developed, commercialized technology. While there have, indeed, been instances of cost overruns, inefficiency, and dominance of pork-barrel politics (the Cresap case comes to mind), many of the pilot plants have perhaps been judged by an unduly harsh standard. In development of novel defense technologies it has traditionally been assumed that one standard of efficiency is required for judging production and another for prototype development. In the case of DCL this seems not to have been the case. In large measure, this rigidity has to do with the fact that the concern, throughout the history of DCL development, has been with the establishment of an industry rather that just the establishment of the technology (see argument below).

In some respects the most important object lesson for the development of coal liquefaction is the South African SASOL plants. Early on, the South Africans picked a viable technology (presumably they could have picked among several), invested heavily with no expectation of quick return, nourished the technology, were patient with early operational problems, and supported the cost of the resultant fuel. This same option was, theoretically, open to the United States, but the United States chose instead to provide for much more limited development of a variety of technologies, none with sustained effort. The bad experiences with many of the pilot plants constructed in the United States have not, in fact, been that different from the early experiences of the South Africans with the SASOL plants. But the South Africans committed to the technology with the result that it had long-term payoff. While there are several problems with the South African analogy,[3] one point is clearly relevant: DCL development requires considerable tolerance for the early technical and operational problems associated with pilot plants.

DCL Is Best Viewed as Government-Sheltered High Technology Development

In our view the attempt to develop a DCL-based industry has been well intentioned but, in some respects, misguided. At this point, and into the immediate future, synthetic fuels options of virtually every variety are best viewed from the standpoint of energy security. DCL is not presently important from a market standpoint, but it is important as a public good, in the same sense that national defense is provided as a public good. It is impossible to put a price on the value of national defense, and it is not reasonable to seek to match the provision of national defense services and products to a competitive market. The public goods characteristics of DCL are considerable. Energy security has enormous "spillover effects"; it defies conventional pricing and confers benefits not easily captured in full by investors and producers. For all of these reasons, reliance on a strategy of industry development and price competition is wrongheaded.

This is not to say that government should seek a monopoly over DCL and become the primary developer. Industry is needed to produce DCL but not for the sake of developing a product that rises or falls in the competitive market. DCL development is not unlike nuclear submarine development. The ludicrousness of requiring defense contractors to market nuclear submarines to private consumers is clear enough. However, there has been no hesitation in expecting that DCL should deliver products that will be marketed chiefly to private consumers. The problem is that the chief value at this point is not to any particular set of consumers but to all consumers and that value is not just fuel but energy security.

We agree with the prevailing opinion of experts interviewed as a part of this effort that DCL support should be aimed at producing energy reserves and that the government should guarantee the price at a level somewhat commensurate to the value of the product to energy security. From this perspective, the price of petroleum is irrelevant. If we assume that petroleum is finite, or even scarce, then it only remains to judge the collective value of energy security. In our view, that value is quite high, far exceeding the price of petroleum. Supporters for development of DCL should consider these shadow prices and guarantee a price adequate to ensure industry participation.

Technological Progress, But Competitive Failure, of DCL

As oil prices rise, projected costs of producing synfuel from a new planned plant using currently foreseeable technology increase proportionately. No matter how high the price of oil rises—even to $100 per barrel—a new plant built subsequent to arrival of oil at that price will not be economic as investment prospect.[4]

To many observers, the reason behind this technology development failure is pure and simple economics. If you can't produce synthetic fuels for less than natural fuels, then don't waste your money trying.

This explanation is, of course, nothing new or original. As early as the 1950s, the National Petroleum Council (NPC) concluded that synthetic liquids from coal could not compete economically with natural petroleum. In attacking the cost estimates of the R&D program of the U.S. Bureau of Mines, the NPC concluded that:

The need for a synthetic liquid fuel industry in this country is still in the distant future. Since new techniques may be available then, we question the wisdom of the government financing large-scale demonstration plants. (NPC, 1953)[5]

This issue, which has not been addressed, is that despite the four major national policy initiatives aimed at stimulating a synthetic fuel industry in the United States, and despite the several billion dollars spent on this technology since 1944, there has been little meaningful progress toward developing the technology to a commercially competitive status or toward understanding the basic science of the processes and feedstocks associated with the technology.[6,7,8] Process efficiencies have improved, but only slightly, and there have been no major breakthroughs concerning the manufacturing technology or knowledge of coal itself since the problem's earliest days.[9,10]

There has been the lack of progress in the technology, which has been the principal barrier to development. The interviews conducted for this book put the blame for this failure directly on lack of fundamental understanding of the raw material: coal. We simply do not know enough about coal at the submolecular-to-atomic level to unravel the basic material into commercially valuable products at an expenditure of energy and hydrogen and at an economic cost that makes the products affordable.

EXPLANATION FOR SYNTHETIC FUEL TECHNOLOGY FAILURE

In an effort to understand better the difficulties associated with the national effort to develop DCL, a review of competing explanations for the failure to develop the technology is required. The various explanations are well known and have often been advanced individually as the principal reason for the difficulties and failures associated with demonstrating DCL. Each is briefly reviewed below.

The Price of Oil: The Moving Target

Petroleum is a commodity with low production costs that is highly supply/demand inelastic in character. This implies that by its very nature

petroleum is a commodity with unique supply and demand characteristics. These characteristics, when combined with uncertainties of the
non-U.S. petroleum supply, play an important role in increasing the
uncertainty associated with development of any technology for manufacturing the replacement for petroleum. This uncertainty—particularly in
terms of price and in terms of the financial scale of a synthetic fuel
industry—is so large that standard market-based investment is not possible.[11] The financial risks are simply too great, given the fluctuations in
the price of petroleum. Furthermore, as shown by the Congressional
Research Service,[12] the price of DCL production is at least partially a
function of the price of oil.

This implies that the economics of petroleum production and distribution prohibit the development of synthetic fuels without large-scale government intervention. Given the fact that government intervention in
the synthetic fuel development cycle has only occurred in response to
supply or price fluctuations or in periods of increased central planning,
and given that government efforts have always been terminated upon
stabilization of the petroleum economy, it is fair to conclude that the
economics of petroleum is a critical variable affecting synthetic fuel technology development.

The economics variable, while certainly important from an investment
perspective (i.e., who is going to finance a $3 billion coal liquefaction
plant to produce $55 per barrel synthetic oil when you can buy oil for
$15 per barrel on the spot market?), is important in that it induces
under-investment in R&D related to synthetic fuels. Nelson and Langlois,[13] in their classic article on the economics of technology development and research, clearly demonstrated that industries, when left to
their own devices in a market economy, have little incentive to carry out
basic research. The result is that without government funding of basic
research, it will not occur on a scale sufficient to address the problems.
Thus the economics problem potentially contributes to the problem of
basic knowledge production. This point is particularly important for
DCL development. Because of the nature of the economics of petroleum
(i.e., the unpredictability of supply, and price fluctuations), government
intervention has focused on the goal of rapid development, commercialization, and production of a petroleum replacement. The result has
been that production of basic knowledge has never had consistent
funding.

Synthetic Fuels Technology Policy: Politics, Pork, and Panic

The shaping of public policy designed to stimulate the development of
DCL and synthetic fuels in general has been a process fraught with

problems. These problems have included: (1) the tendency to under-utilize scientific and technical information in DCL R&D decisions[14]; (2) the use of demonstration plants as a means of political risk versus technical risk reduction[15]; (3) the multiple policy goals associated with DCL development[16]; (4) the inability of government to pick "winning" technologies[17]; and (5) the general problem of goal setting in the DCL policy arena.[18]

When considered collectively, the problems associated with DCL policymaking distill down to the fact that government has often attempted to do too much, without enough information, in an effort to address different and often conflicting goals. It is simply impossible to set production goals for a DCL technology that lacks a knowledge base beyond its first generation and lacks the operating experience from which realistic expectations can be developed. In addition, when the siting of the demonstration plants is a function of political geography as much as it is a function of engineering criteria, it can be expected that there will be goal conflict problems and technical tradeoffs that could jeopardize the technical success and ultimately the economics of the process.

Premature Development: Too Much Development and Not Enough Research

By the late 1980s, the United States has yet to demonstrate a commercially viable synthetic fuel process. This lack of success wasn't the result of insufficient funding or an inadequate time frame. For example, President Ford's initial commitment to DCL and synthetic fuel was made in 1975 with the Project Independence effort. The lack of developmental success is a function of the fact that pre-development research for DCL was lacking.[19]

Resources Have Been Spread Too Thin: Small Increments Spread out over Multiple Projects

In an assessment of the South African SASOL development experience, Olliver concludes with the following observation:

It is just as well that Sasol plunged ahead with a big plant; if it had been cautious and dabbled with a pilot plant, the problems and the change in the outlook for oil would probably have killed the project, and there would be no process in the world that could, if needed, be relied upon to produce oil from coal without many years of development.[20]

The U.S. approach has been small-scale support of multiple projects rather than large-scale support of one or two major projects. While we are not prepared to argue that it has been a mistake to hedge bets and to continue to develop multiple technologies, we do suggest that the failure to commit to one or two (in addition to small-scale investments in several) is the best explanation of why no plant currently exists.

There are a number of reasons for the tendency toward multiple small-scale developments. In the first place, it was never assumed during any of the growth periods for DCL that funding would dry up so completely or so quickly. Just as important, the politics of the pork barrel almost always dictate that more is better. Few federal programs and projects are not subject to the demands of distributional politics. More to the point, the chief political currency of DCL projects, especially at early stages, is regional economic impact. It is usually easier, politically, to provide for many small-scale regional impacts than for one or two projects with gigantic impact. Indeed, sometimes relatively small-scale regional economic impacts are more desirable than gigantic ones because they are beneficial but less disruptive. Thus, purely from the standpoint of distributional politics, it is "rational" to provide as many projects as practically feasible, given a particular level of investment.

There are many DCL technologies that "work." The tradeoffs for each vary—some are not so cheap, others are not so clean, still others are less proven—but several seem at least equal to the processes used for years in the SASOL plants. It would seem to make sense to choose one or two of the best currently available technologies and provide a sustained developmental effort while continuing to support other approaches at a—relatively—more modest level.

Invest in Contingency Planning

The events influencing DCL development have been, from one perspective at least, unpredictable. However, it can also be argued that the possible scenarios affecting DCL have been and are presently knowable. As mentioned above, few people in the early and mid-1970s would have predicted that there would soon be an oil glut and that the need for a DCL alternative would seem so much less compelling. But the discontinuities and rapid change associated with the DCL economic and policy environments need not wreak havoc to the extent they have in the past.

Contingency planning is one key to dealing with an environmental setting likely to continue to be unstable and volatile. Contingency planning, properly implemented, could smooth some of the disruptions caused by changes in course. Naturally, more stable policies would be welcome, but it is best to proceed as if policies will not be stable. Contingency planning might provide a set of workable development alternatives for any of a variety of specified environmental conditions. While contingency planning would, in principle, provide considerable benefits in rationalizing DCL developmental efforts, it must be underscored that contingency plans are useful only to the extent that they are taken seriously and implemented. Perhaps the best approach to formulating contingency plans for DCL development is through some forum drawing together researchers, industry, and public policymakers to advise on the most appropriate directions, given various levels of resources and national need. Only if all major parties to DCL development participate in contingency planning is there any strong likelihood that contingency plans will be implemented during periods of major environmental change. Moreover, the most likely benefit of a thorough-going contingency planning effort is not the direct product, which may or may not be implemented, but the exercise itself. One failure in DCL policy has been the inability of policymakers and other actors to anticipate some of the major environmental shocks that have affected DCL development. The very process of anticipating possible changes might itself prove valuable. This report, providing a retrospective assessment of DCL development, might well be the first step in a more formal, multi-party contingency planning effort.

THE HIATUS EFFECT AND DCL

Significance of the Hiatus Effect

With the demise of the Synthetic Fuels Corporation (SFC) in 1985,[21] the 90 percent reduction of federal synthetic fuel research funding since 1981, and the post-1982[22] shutdown of the major synthetic fuels research labs in industry, the United States ended its fourth major[23] synthetic fuels technology development thrust in this century, without having demonstrated the commercial viability of a single process configuration.

It is fair to assume that the development failure associated with DCL in the United States is at least partially explained by the economics of oil, the sectoral coordination problems described by Vietor, and the politics of the energy crisis.[24] An explanation as to why these problems became more pervasive in the case of DCL development than in the case of other macro-engineering technologies is needed if an improved understanding of large-scale technology development processes is to be developed and if the potential of DCL is to be more accurately assessed.

In addition to these broadly discussed problem areas associated with DCL development, there was the major problem of discontinuous scientific and engineering activity associated with the technology. In effect, DCL development in the United States has experienced several major hiatuses where little or no significant research, development, or demonstration was carried out or where insufficient time and effort were devoted to the technology. These hiatus periods were the product of incon-sistent public policy[25] and under-investment in basic research by in-dustry and government, and had the result of limiting the potential of DCL as a fuel replacement option.

Given the fact that the United States has just entered its third major technology development hiatus, it is important that the potential effect of these periods on the future of DCL be understood prior to the initia-tion of any future research development and demonstration (RD&D) program.

DCL processes, as conceptualized in the periods of U.S. development, were not competitive given the price of oil and the market economics of large petroleum/energy companies. The result was that each effort to develop DCL ended in failure. But does this explanation indicate why the technology itself failed? The answer is no.

Recent analyses by the Rand Corporation indicate that a critical vari-able in the success of any process-oriented technology is the continuous support of an R&D program over an extended period of time.[26] Discon-tinuous support or breaks in the process development cycle, labeled the hiatus effect, was viewed as the most critical factor in determining the success probability of process type technologies, such as DCL. Further-more, an analysis of information/knowledge survival rates, both in pri-vate firms and the government, suggests that information and knowl-edge regarding process technologies, such as DCL, are often lost during periods of non-R&D activity. This loss factor appears to be a function of the extent to which new demonstration and pilot plant knowledge is produced on a continuous basis. Another important factor identified by the Rand team is the importance of person-to-person knowledge trans-fer in this type of R&D effort. Apparently, after an R&D team is dis-mantled and assigned new duties, the loss rate of knowledge is very high.

In addition to the effect of hiatus periods on the loss of information and knowledge important to the development cycle, Hess concluded that the improvement of plant performance in process-oriented technology is a function of continuous incremental improvements.[27] Using the SASOL I experience, it is estimated that it takes four to five years to eliminate basic performance problems in innovative pioneer plans. According to Hess, "This suggests that, for an innovative technology, a second plant poten-tially faces fewer start-up difficulties if its design does not begin until after the pioneer plant has had at least 5 years operational experience."[28] Given this initial time investment, the Rand study further concludes that an additional ten to fifteen years of pioneer plant operation is frequently required. Any hiatus period in this twenty-year cycle will significantly diminish the potential of any improvements to reduce the process cost and potentially limit the viability of the technology.

In a related study, Lieberman found that a continuous and higher level of R&D expenditures accelerates the rate of process improvement.[29] Discontinuous R&D, it is speculated, has the effect of reducing and limiting the rate of process improvement. Using patents only in the area of coal liquids production, Table 9.1 details the change in the patents rate after the 1974 and 1980 funding patterns changes and illustrates the drastic changes in patent productivity in these periods.

Regarding the overall effect of hiatus periods in the R&D process, Myers and Arguden concluded that time, as opposed to people, facilities, or information storage systems, was the critical variable in determining the decay rate of process-oriented knowledge.[30] Their consensus seemed to be that delays in the twenty-year cycle would require reinitiation of the development effort after each extended hiatus.

While the effects of periods of hiatus on the production of basic knowledge are difficult to measure, it is known that funding reduction pattern does affect the rate and direction of knowledge production.[31] Given this reduction in the rate of production and the fact that diminution in the rate of knowledge production can result in a dissemination problem, it is speculated that periods of research hiatus result in excessive research duplication and reinitiation. These reinitiation efforts are often time consuming and lead to substantial delays in technology development processes. Beyond the knowledge losses, there is the more general effect of limiting the search for potentially new processes that might be based on the findings of the basic research.

In sum, the hiatus effect on technology development engenders a reduction in the ability of a process to develop along standard cost-reducing routes. The process development cycle appears to be about twenty years for significant cost reductions to occur and for technical risk to be reduced to levels that will permit investment.

Table 9.1.
Approximate Development Cycle for the Coal Liquefaction Option of Synthetic Fuels Technology

Hiatus Period 3	1985–	Nearly complete Research, Development and Demonstration Program shutdown
Premature attempt	1980–85	Organization of the synthetic Fuels to commercialize Corporation DCL
Premature demonstration	1976–80	Synthetic Fuels Commercial Demonstration program
	1974–77	Coal Con Demonstration Failure

(*continued*)

Table 9.1. (Continued)

Premature development	1963–74	OCR develops and operates 3 liquefaction pilot plants (projects racked by funding and development problems)
	1961	Office of Coal Research (OCR) established in the U.S. Department of the Interior. Small scale coal research/synthetic fuels research initiated
Hiatus Period 2	1952–56	Carbide and Carbon Chemicals operates a 300 ton/day hydrogenation plant after 17 years of lab scale work.
	1953	U.S. pilot plant in Louisiana, MO, shut down after running six American coals. Cost studies show process not competitive.
	1949	First U.S. hydrogenation pilot plant began operation in Louisiana, MO.
Hiatus Period 1	1945	New U.S. Bureau of Mines liquefaction lab erected at Bruceton, PA
	1941–44	12 million metric tons of synthetic liquids produced from first-generation plants in Germany
	1936–44	11 first-generation plants built and operated by Germans
	1936	U.S. Bureau of Mines initiates experimental work on coal liquefaction
Premature Development	1927–36	Operation of Leuna liquefaction plant
	1927	First-generation hydrogenation demonstration plant built in Europe
	1920s	Germans discover 3 processes for coal conversion to liquid fuels
	1924	U.S. Bureau of Mines initiates small scale coal synthesis research

Additional hiatus effects include a reduction in the rate of production of new knowledge and, thus, a reduction in the probability of developing new pioneer process configurations.

The Hiatus Effect in DCL Development

The development of DCL appears historically to have been done in a rush in response to a critical national need. As early as the 1920s, German coal hydrogenation R&D efforts were carried out with great haste, almost in a crisis environment. It wasn't until 1925 that Pier obtained a good quality gasoline from coal,[32] and this was only at the bench scale. By September 1926 a plan to construct a 100,000-ton processing plant at Leuna had been developed and was announced.[33] Completed after a monumental effort in 1927, the plant was fraught with technical difficulties and cost overruns. Production never reached more than 70,000 tons at the Leuna plant (before 1929), and according to the developers (I. G. Farber),[34] the plant was so expensive that more R&D was needed before moving ahead with any other plants. Despite arguments to shut down Leuna and put a moratorium on R&D, development continued. This continued effort was carried out as a means of potentially developing raw materials to aid in the balance of payments problem Germany faced at the time.

Changes in the petroleum market between 1926 and 1930 forced the process developers to focus on development of internal markets and ultimately after 1933 development for the support of Weimar government policies, including rearmament. Thus, the development of the eleven additional coal hydrogenation plants (between 1936 and 1943) for the production of synthetic gasoline "flourished in an environment of rearmament and autarky."[35]

From a technology development perspective, the German experience between 1927 and 1944 could be classified as a first-generation technology demonstration. Unfortunately, the plants were never intended to be competitive on the world market, and perhaps more importantly, they were not based on a sound knowledge base. These German plants were also never fully developed in the sense that they lacked a systematic research development and demonstration history over the twenty-year time frame suggested by Rand. They did operate but very inefficiently and with numerous technical difficulties.

In the period between 1945 and 1948, U.S. efforts to capitalize on the German first-generation DCL knowledge were launched in response to a perceived oil supply crisis. This plan, however, was based on several incorrect assumptions, not the least of which was the effect of the knowledge loss rate in transferring the German technology base to the United States after the war. These mistakes included:

1. the assumption that the German technology was sound because it had worked, when in fact, from an economic perspective, it was not viable;

2. the assumption that the empirically developed German hydrogenation process could easily covert to U.S. coal characteristics, when it was the variation in coal chemistry itself that was the major cause of difficulty at Leuna and the other plants.

U.S. policy in the 1940s had embarked on the path of demonstrating an unproven, uneconomical technology that lacked the scientific base necessary for improvements. The result was an unsuccessful four-year operation of the hydrogenation pilot plant in Louisiana, Missouri.

In the case of the Louisiana, Missouri, pilot plant, the hiatus effect begins to impact significantly on the DCL process. There had been only limited U.S. R&D on hydrogenation since the 1920s, with only three to four years of significant research before the beginning of the 1949 demonstration.[36] Thus, the U.S. data base was limited and the German data base was certainly spotty at best. Beyond the research base inadequacies, the pilot plant was only operated for four years before complete shutdown. According to the Rand studies, this would have been an insufficient time period to develop the technology further and lower the costs. Following the shutdown of the plant in 1953, with the exception of some small-scale industrial efforts, the U.S. DCL development program entered a ten-year period of minimal research and development. Such a hiatus would indicate that in 1963, when the Office of Coal Research (OCR) began the development of three liquefaction demonstration projects, the technology development process had returned almost to square one.

The result was that once again, as was the case in 1929 with the Leuna plant and in 1949 with the U.S. project, the demonstration projects were overwhelmed by cost overruns and economic efficiency problems. By 1974 when the political cry for DCL development began in response to the Arab oil embargo, no demonstration project of the OCR had yet been successful. While there are certainly numerous factors that contributed to the lack of success of these demonstration efforts, it is our contention that the principal reason for failure was the fact that the projects were sold as demonstrations of a proven technology when in fact they were attempts to demonstrate a technology that was never designed to be economical and had already suffered two major periods of non-development—the German–U.S. transfer after World War II and the 1953–1963 U.S. funding gap.

In 1974, out of panic and in an attempt by OCR to protect its bureaucratic status, a major demonstration project was funded. Known as Coalcon, the project suffered immediately from cost overruns and technical failure. In fact, it is not unfair to conclude that the decision to

2. What are the unknowns and potential problems? For example:
   • process dynamics and control of the two-step system;
   • material handling.
E. Can we effectively model the significant processes today? If not, what additional information must be obtained to model the process to permit computer simulation to test, for example, sensitivity to process changes?
F. To what extent is the compatibility of DCL product with refinery operations a significant problem?
   1. Necessary changes to refinery operations to accommodate DCL product?
   2. How does the energy loss in refining DCL product compare with refining natural crude, for a comparable product slate? (Quoted DCL thermal efficiencies don't take such losses into account.)
G. If the price of oil were $30/bbl today and climbing, what would be the most significant problems in commercializing each of the major existing processes?

III. NEW INITIATIVES

Is our best chance to advance direct liquefaction through new approaches? What should our objectives in direct liquefaction be?

A. Where is the real leverage on product cost?
   1. Pressure and temperature reduction?
   2. Slurry handling?
   3. Catalyst improvement?
      Some researchers feel that major improvements can still be made in catalysts. Examples include:
      • iron complexes (e.g., ferrocene, iron pentacarbonyl);
      • mixed metals: synergistic effects are claimed;
      • transition metals (West Virginia is the proponent);
      • site-specific and/or bond-specific catalysts.

Comment?

   4. H_2 production/consumption?
   5. Co-processing with heavy oil?
      It has been observed that addition of coal to residual oil and other heavy oils during upgrading operations strongly inhibits coking and aids in segregating their high metal content with the processing residue. It is suggested that this approach could:
      a. reduce process equipment cost and complexity by eliminating or reducing the need to produce solvent from the DCL product;
      b. increase the value of the DCL process by processing heavy oils as well as coal;
      c. improve process chemistry because the presence of heavy oils seems to accelerate the liquefaction reaction. We don't know why, but one speculation is that the metals in the oil act as catalysts.

6. Coal characterization/beneficiation/fractionation?
7. Bioengineering?
8. Improved understanding of DCL chemistry?
   Many researchers feel that understanding of DCL reaction chemistry is still inadequate, in areas such as reaction intermediates and catalytically active sites. What more is there to learn, and how might it help us in improving actual processes?

B. What knowledge streams or sources (journals, conferences, etc.) do you consider most significant in advancing DCL?

C. To what degree is DCL being pursued in private sector R&D? What type of research is being done? What does the research focus on:
   1. Incremental improvements to existing processes?
   2. New and substantially different processes?
   3. Basic scientific work on process chemistry and mechanisms?
   4. Bench-scale development of new processes?
   5. Process development unit-scale development of new processes?

IV. ECONOMICS: COMPETITION WITH OTHER FUELS AND FUNDING NEEDS

A. What can be done to make direct liquefaction competitive? How would DCL be commercialized if and when it is needed, given the fundamental instability of oil prices? The most effective steps would be:
   1. Government subsidy
   2. Use the most reactive coal available
   3. Coprocessing at an existing refinery

B. Will indirect liquefaction (coal gasification) provide significant competition to DCL? Electric utilities will probably be using coal gasification combined cycle plants within the next decade. How much advantage does this give indirect liquefaction? Should we be pursuing DCL processes that could be integrated with gasifier power plants (e.g., take the easily extractable liquids and then feed the coal to the gasification plant for electric power). Use the gasification plant as a source for hydrogen.

C. Methanol from fermentation?

D. Ethanol from fermentation?

E. Are there other transportable fuel manufacturing options that will significantly impact the commercial viability of DCL? For example, production of hydrocarbon materials from plants.

F. Does basic research deserve more relative funding as opposed to demonstrations or do we need to persevere with demonstration plants, make incremental improvements, and gain experience?

G. Have DCL plant and product costs tended to increase with world oil prices?
   1. How reliable are the projected costs of commercial DCL plants and products as presented in various DOE reports?
   2. It appears that through the 1970s, commercial cost estimates rose in rough proportion to oil prices, presenting a "receding" horizon

situation in which DCL could not compete regardless of the price of oil. Is this a function of a real linkage between DCL plant construction costs and the cost of oil, or simply coincidence? Comments?
3. Why was DCL unsuccessful in obtaining Synthetic Fuel Corp. demonstration project funding, as compared to other options such as oil shale?

V. POLICY QUESTIONS

A. To some extent the development of DCL may be a function of the policy priorities of the administrations of various U.S. presidents. Sometimes changes in energy policy affect DCL development, sometimes other policies—defense, economic policy—might affect DCL, at least indirectly. For as many presidential administrations as you have knowledge, going back to the Eisenhower administration and forward to the Reagan administration, please tell us, first: the major energy policy changes that affect DCL development; and second: the other major policies that affected DCL development:
   • Energy policies under Presidents Eisenhower, Kennedy, Johnson, Nixon, Ford, Carter, Reagan.
   • Non-energy presidential policies under presidents.
B. Sometimes particular individuals in government agencies have an impact on energy policy apart from simply implementing the president's priorities. For example, a head of the OCR or an assistant secretary at DOE may be especially concerned with coal liquefaction or some other set of energy policies. Are there such members of the executive branch, working in federal agencies, who have played an especially significant role in shaping DCL development? We are concerned with the period from the early 1950s to the present. Please be specific about particular individuals and their particular impacts on DCL policy.
C. Likewise, congressional actors sometimes play a major role in energy policy and perhaps even DCL development. Can you think of any senators or U.S. representatives who had a particularly important impact on DCL development policy since the beginning of the Eisenhower administration?
D. To what extent, over the years, has DCL policy been viewed as an issue related to national defense and national security? Has this affected DCL development in an important way?
E. To what extent has DCL been a political pork-barrel issue, that is, a means for politicians to win favor with constituents by having public works projects built in their districts? Please be specific.

Finally: Now that you have a good idea of the purposes and interests of our study, can you give us a question we should have asked but didn't?

APPENDIX II

TELEPHONE INTERVIEW PROTOCOL: HISTORY, PRESENT STATUS, AND NEW DIRECTIONS IN DIRECT COAL LIQUEFACTION
(Includes expanded policy questions)

I. INTRODUCTION

Our Goals

Identify the best research and policy approaches to commercializing DCL.

A. Technical leverage points to improve economics. Fundamental limitations of DCL.
B. Understand the industrial and knowledge resources available to advance DCL. Deficiencies and their implications?
C. Gain perspective on the role of DCL as a future energy source, if it has any. Most likely routes to commercial use?

Our Approach

Compile and analyze expert judgment on the state and prospects of DCL technology:

A. Patterns that promoted and/or impeded progress historically.
B. Main constraints on cost and performance of existing DCL processes.
   Leverage points and research directions that could exploit them.
   Basic physical limitations, if any.
C. State of current DCL R&D:
   1. Private sector activities and attitudes,
   2. Major research teams and directions,

3. Significant technical and business trends.
Identify steps that could be taken to enhance the contribution of these activities toward ultimate DCL commercialization.

D. Competing technologies and their status.

II. GENERAL QUESTIONS

A. What is your present involvement in DCL research? Why are you involved?

B. Who are the major research players? Their directions and stakes?
   • incremental improvements to existing processes?
   • new and substantially different processes?
   • basic scientific work on process chemistry and mechanisms?

C. Who are the major commercial players? Their direction and stakes?

D. Generally, how would you characterize the state of DCL technology?
   • technically well understood or not?
   • potential for major process advancement versus "nibbling away"?
   • economics and potential for improvement?

E. What are our present capabilities to model DCL
   1. Process design and performance?
   2. Economics?
   3. Integration of process and economics? (E.g., repeated interview comments that we need to "optimize" rather than maximize yield: trade off some yield for reduced cost.)
      • Are present capabilities adequate?
      • What improvements are needed?
      • How would improvements be beneficial?

F. If the price of oil were $30/bbl today and climbing, what would be the most significant problems in commercializing DCL?

G. What should our main technical objectives be for DCL? Where is the real leverage on product cost?

H. How important was information exchange among DCL researchers during the post-1973 "push"?
   1. Exchange among pilot plant and demo projects
   2. Exchange between lab research and pilot/demo projects. What were the main mechanisms? Was the exchange adequate?

III. NEW INITIATIVES

A number of new directions in DCL research have been proposed. We would like to review them briefly and get your views on their potential.

A. "Supersolvents" reportedly could dramatically reduce process severity.
   • EPRI originally involved in research
   • main problem is separating from process residue economically.

B. Improved catalysts
   Some researchers feel that major improvements can be made.
   Examples:
   - iron complexes (e.g., ferrocene, iron pentacarbonyl);
   - mixed metals: synergistic effects are claimed;
   - transition metals (West Virginia is the proponent);
   - site-specific and/or bond-specific catalysts.
C. Co-processing with heavy oil? It is suggested that this approach could:
   1. Reduce process equipment cost and complexity by eliminating or reducing the need to produce solvent from the DCL product.
   2. Increase the value of the DCL process by processing heavy oils as well as coal.
   3. Improve process chemistry because the presence of heavy oils seems to accelerate the liquefaction reaction. We don't know why, but one speculation is that the metals in the oil act as catalysts.
D. Optimization of existing processes
   It is suggested that DCL economics can be improved by optimizing yield rather than maximizing it: that is, accepting lower yield in return for lower cost. Residuals might also contribute some value.
E. Coal characterization/beneficiation/fractionation? The existence of coal maceral components that dissolve more readily (e.g., resinite in Utah coals) suggests selecting the coal based on the presence of these components, and possibly separating them out (either physically or by solvent extraction) and liquefying them only.
F. Bioengineering? Is there any evidence that we can get biological organisms that will liquefy coal, not just beneficiate it for conventional DCL?
G. Improved understanding of DCL reaction chemistry. Many researchers feel that understanding of DCL reaction chemistry is still inadequate:
   - reaction intermediates
   - catalytically active sites
   What more is there to learn, and how might it help us to improve actual processes?

IV. ECONOMICS: COMPETITION WITH OTHER FUELS AND FUNDING NEEDS

A. What can be done to make direct liquefaction competitive? How would DCL be commercialized if and when it is needed, given the fundamental instability of oil prices?
B. What use, if any, do utilities have for DCL? Does utility pursuit of gasification make indirect liquefaction a more likely route? How does methanol production from IGCC plants fit in? Can DCL be integrated beneficially with IGCC plants?
C. Ethanol, methanol?
D. Are there other transportable fuel manufacturing options that will

significantly impact the commercial viability of DCL? For example, production of hydrocarbon materials from plants?

E. Have DCL plant and product costs tended to increase with world oil prices? Why? How does this relate to future efforts to commercialize DCL?

F. How reliable are current projected costs of commercial DCL plants and products as presented in various DOE reports?

G. Why was DCL unsuccessful in obtaining Synthetic Fuel Corp. demonstration project funding, as compared to other options such as oil shale?

H. Does basic research deserve more relative funding as opposed to demonstrations, or do we need to persevere with demonstration plants, make incremental improvements, and gain experience?

V. POLICY QUESTIONS

To some extent, the development of DCL may be a function of the policy priorities of the administrations of various U.S. presidents. Also, particular individuals in federal government agencies, Congress, and the states may have an impact. In addition to energy policy, per se, other federal policies such as defense and economic policy may be important. The purpose of this series of questions is to identify:

• Major federal policies that have shaped DCL development, and their effects, positive and negative.

• Policy options that could enhance further DCL development, and their likely impacts.

A. Questions on policies that shaped DCL development:
1. For as many presidential administrations as you have knowledge, going back to the Eisenhower administration and forward to the Reagan administration, please tell us:
   a. the major energy policy changes that affect DCL development under Presidents Eisenhower, Kennedy, Johnson, Nixon, Ford, Carter, Reagan.
   b. Other major policies that affected DCL development.
2. Particular individuals in agencies may have had an impact on energy policy apart from simply implementing the president's priorities. For example, a head of the OCR or an assistant secretary at DOE may be especially concerned with coal liquefaction or some other set of energy policies. Are there such members of the executive branch, working in federal agencies, who have played an especially significant role in shaping DCL development? We are concerned with the period from the early 1950s to the present. Please be specific about particular individuals and ther particular impacts on DCL policy.
3. Likewise, congressional actors sometimes play a major role in energy policy and perhaps even DCL development. Can you think of any

senators or U.S. representatives who had a particularly important impact on DCL development policy since the beginning of the Eisenhower administration?

4. To what extent, over the years, has DCL policy been viewed as an issue related to national defense and national security? Has this affected DCL development in an important way?

5. To what extent has DCL been a political pork-barrel issue, that is, a means for politicians to win favor with constituents by having public works projects built in their districts? Please be specific.

6. The H-Coal has not reached commercial readiness and has not been supported consistently:
   - In 1967, OCR terminated research support for H-coal in favor of project gasoline (IDCL) because it was seen as nearer to commercial readiness.
   - The Breckinridge "commercial" H-coal project never got off the ground. Ashland pulled out, citing "economic grounds."

What lessons are there in this experience for DCL development policy? Was it simply an "economic" problem?

B. Questions on policy for future DCL development:

1. To what extent do you think it might be possible for various political action groups such as the National Coal Association or the Synfuels Organization to influence support for DCL?

2. What other groups are/might be important in this regard? Coal companies? Oil companies? OTA? CRS? and so forth.

3. Are you active in these groups? Are you aware of their current lobbying interests or direction in terms of research?

4. What events, if any, might mobilize interest groups to support action for DCL? Tax advantage, government markets, other markets, declare a national emergency?

5. To what extent do you think the current tax code encourages development of DCL? What changes might encourage development?

6. Recently, what political actors, in Congress, the states, or federal agencies, have been especially prominent in supporting DCL?

7. Are there particular factors that seem to determine whether a political actor will be motivated to work either for or against a DCL political agenda?
   - regional?
   - economic?
   - political, geopolitical?
   - ties to oil companies?
   - general interest in technical issues?
   - committee assignments?
   - political party?

8. Have you, as an individual or a member of an organized group, been active in seeking additional political support for DCL? What form has

that action taken? Has it been successful? If you have not been active, how might you be mobilized?

9. Is there a need for a national energy policy? How does DCL fit in? What should its priority be versus other alternatives? How should the problem of unstable petroleum prices be addressed?

Finally: Now that you have a good idea of the purposes and interests of our study, can you give us a question we should have asked but didn't?

——————————————— *NOTES*

Preface

1. J. F. Coates, "Technology Assessment: A Tool Kit," Chemtech (June 1976): 372.

2. Mary Hamilton, "The Use of Historical Records to Inform Prospective Technology Assessments," in J. Tarr, *Retrospective Technology Assessment* (San Francisco: San Francisco Press, 1976): 5–6.

Chapter 1

1. R. W. Hess, "Review of Cost Improvement Literature with Emphasis on Synthetic Fuel Facilities and the Petroleum and Chemical Process Industry." Santa Monica, CA: Rand Corp., March 1985.

2. U. Desai and M. Crow, "Failures of Power and Intelligence in Government Decision-Making: The Case of Coalcon," *Administration and Society* 15, no. 2 (1983): 185–206.

3. R. Shangraw, *H-Coal: A Technology Policy Case Study* (Syracuse, NY: The Maxwell School, Syracuse University, 1982), mimeo.

4. B. Bozeman, "Retrospective Technology Assessment Methodology: Integrating Qualitative and Quantitative Approaches." Paper prepared for the International Forecasting Society, Paris, France, 1986. J. Tarr (ed.), *Retrospective Technology Assessment* (San Francisco: San Francisco Press, 1977).

5. For an overview, see R. Vietor, "The Synthetic Liquid Fuels Program: Energy Politics in the Truman Era," *Business History Review* 54, no. 1 (1980): 1–34.

6. As used here, the term "technology development environment" refers to the relevant social setting of a technology and includes variables pertaining to market conditions, public perceptions, policy priorities, the nature of the con-

temporary policy agenda, industry structure and orientation and so forth, as these factors interact with the characteristics of the technology itself.

7. For an overview, see R. Vietor, *Energy Policy in America Since 1945* (New York: Cambridge University Press, 1984).

8. See M. Crow, "U.S. Synthetic Fuels Development: The Impact of the Reagan Administration." Syracuse, NY: Technology and Information Policy Program, Syracuse University, 1984.

Chapter 2

1. E. Q. Daddario, Chairman, Subcommittee on Science, Research, and Development of the Committee on Science and Astronautics, U.S. House of Representatives, 90th Congress, 1st Session, Series 1 (Revised, August 1968).

2. B. Bozeman and F. A. Rossini, "Technology Assessment and Political Decisionmaking," *Technological Forecasting and Social Change* 10, no. 2 (1981).

3. J. P. Martino, *Technological Forecasting for Decision Making* (New York: American Elsevier, 1972).

4. See, for example, G. Wise, "The Accuracy of Technological Forecasts, 1890–1940," *Futures* 88, no. 5 (1976): 411–419.

5. Joel Tarr (ed.), *Retrospective Technology Assessment—1976* (San Francisco: San Francisco Press, 1977).

6. These include Ithiel de Sola Pool, *Forecasting the Telephone: A Retrospective Technology Assessment* (Norwood, NJ: Ablex Publishing, 1983); V. T. Coates and Bernard Finn, *A Retrospective Technology Assessment: Submarine Telegraphy* (San Francisco: San Francisco Press, 1982).

7. See, for example, L. White, Jr., "Technology Assessment from the Stance of a Medieval Historian," *American Historical Review* 79, no. 1 (1974): 1–13.

8. There are several general treatments of technology assessment that provide this information. These include A. L. Porter, F. A. Rossini, S. R. Carpenter, and A. T. Roper, *A Guidebook for Technology Assessment and Impact Analysis* (New York: North Holland, 1980); S. Arnstein and A. Christakis (eds.), *Perspectives on Technology Assessment* (Jerusalem: Science and Technology Publishers, 1975); F. Hetman, *Society and the Assessment of Technology* (Paris: OECD, 1973).

9. J. F. Coates, "Technology Assessment: A Tool Kit," Chemtech (June 1976): 372.

10. Richard Carpenter, "The Scope and Limits of Technology Assessment." OECD Seminar on Technology Assessment, Paris (January 26–28, 1972): 1–2.

11. Porter, et al., *A Guidebook for Technology Assessment,* op. cit.

12. M. V. Jones, *A Comparative State-of-the-Art Review of Selected U.S. Technology Assessment Studies* (Washington, D.C.: The Mitre Corporation, 1973).

13. See, for example, T. J. Gordon, "Cross Impact Matrices: An Illustration of Their Use for Policy Analysis," *Futures* 2 (1969): 527–531; D. W. Malone, "An Overview of Interpretative Structural Modeling," in S. Arnstein and A. Christakis, *Perspectives on Technology Assessment* (Jerusalem: Science and Technology Publishers, 1975): 229–233.

14. Except, of course, with the application of the law-like assumptions that underpin the physical sciences, assumptions not appropriate to technology as-

sessment. For elaboration of this point, see B. Bozeman, "The Epistemology of Futures Studies," *Public Administration Review* (1977).

15. See M. R. Hamilton, "The Use of Historical Records to Inform Prospective Technology Assessments," in Tarr (ed.), *Retrospective Technology Assessment— 1976,* op. cit., pp. 5–14.

16. For an elaboration of this approach, see B. Bozeman, "The Credibility of Policy Analysis," *Policy Studies Journal* (June 1986).

17. See, for example, M. Turoff, *The Delphi Method* (New York: American Elsevier, 1977).

18. I. L. White, "Interdisciplinarity," in S. Arnstein and A. Christakis, *Perspectives on Technology Assessment,* op. cit., pp. 87–96; J. F. Coates, "Interdisciplinary Considerations in Sponsoring TA's," *Technology Assessment* 1, no. 2 (1978): 109–120; D. N. Michale, M. R. Berg, and R. Rich. *Research on the Utilization of Technology Assessment Studies* (Ann Arbor: Center for Research on Utilization of Scientific Knowledge, 1976).

19. Porter et al., *A Guidebook,* op. cit.; J. B. Taylor, "Building an Interdisciplinary Team," in Arnstein and Christakis, *Perspectives,* op. cit.

20. For a discussion of approaches to integrating technology assessment perspectives, see F. A. Rossini, S. R. Carpenter, J. Havick, P. Kelly, M. Lipscomb, and A. L. Porter, *Frameworks and Factors Affecting Integration Within Technology Assessments,* Report to the National Science Foundation (Atlanta, Georgia: Institute of Technology, 1978).

21. National Academy of Engineering, "Processes of Assessment and Choice," Washington, D.C.: Committee on Science and Astronautics, U.S. House of Representatives, July 1969.

22. The Mitre Corporation, *A Technology Assessment Methodology* (Washington, D.C.: Office of Science and Technology, Executive Office of the President, June 1971).

23. For an enlightening discussion of the need to integrate standard analytical methods with ad hoc problem-oriented designs, see Richard Kulka, "Idiosyncrasy and Circumstance: Choices and Constraints in the Research Process," in J. E. McGrath, J. Martin, and R. A. Kulka, *Judgment Calls in Research* (Beverly Hills, CA: Sage Publishing, 1982).

24. F. A. Rossini, A. L. Porter, and E. Zucker, "Multiple Technology Assessments," *Journal of the International Society for Technology Assessment* 2 (1976): 21–28.

25. Ibid.

26. J. E. Armstrong and W. W. Harmon, "Strategies for Conducting Technology Assessments," Report to the National Science Foundation (Palo Alto, CA: Department of Engineering and Economic Systems, Stanford University, 1977).

27. M. R. Berg, "Methodology," in Arnstein and Christakis, *Perspectives,* op. cit., pp. 63–72.

28. Ithiel de Sola Pool, *Forecasting the Telephone,* op. cit.

29. For some insight into the character of work in the field of history of technology and, by implication, differences with RTA, see Jack Goodwin, "Current Bibliography in the History of Technology," *Technology and Culture, 1964– 1986* (bibliography appears annually); and G. H. Daniels, "The Big Question in the History of American Technology," *Technology and Culture* 11 (1970): 1–21.

30. R. Wik, "Benjamin Hold and the Invention of the Track Type Tractor," *Technology and Culture* 20 (1979): 90–107.

31. L. D. Stephens, "Farish Furman's Formula: Scientific Farming in the New South," *Agricultural History* 50 (1976): 377–390.

32. J. H. Cassedy, "Applied Microscopy and American Diplomacy: Charles Wardell Stiles in Germany," *Isis* 62 (1971): 5–20.

33. Elting Morison, *From Know-how to Nowhere: The Development of American Technology* (New York: Basic Books, 1974).

34. M. R. Hamilton, "The Use of Historical Records to Inform Prospective Technology Assessments," Tarr (ed.), *Retrospective*, op. cit., pp. 5–14.

35. A. L. Porter, "Complexity, Causality, Caveats: Methodological Findings of A Retrospective Technology Assessment," in Tarr (ed.), *Retrospective*, op. cit., pp. 31–54.

36. M. R. Hamilton, in Tarr (ed.), *Retrospective*, op. cit.

37. Ibid., p. 8.

Chapter 3

1. M. R. Hamilton, "The Use of Historical Records to Inform Prospective Technology Assessments," in J. Tarr (ed.), *Retrospective Technology Assessment* (San Francisco: San Francisco Press, 1976): 5–6.

2. B. Bozeman and R. Rossini, "Technology Assessment and Political Decision-making," *Technological Forecasting and Social Change* 15, no. 1 (1979): 25–35.

3. Perhaps the most familiar application of this approach is in Graham Allison's interpretation of the Cuban missile crisis, in *The Essence of Decision*.

4. *Federal Statistics,* Vols. 1–2 (Washington, D.C.: U.S. G.P.O., 1971).

5. See C. W. Churchman, *The Design of Inquiring Systems,* (Chicago: Basic Books, 1971).

6. Carl Hempel, *Philosophy of Natural Science* (Englewood Cliffs, NJ: Prentice-Hall, 1964).

Chapter 4

1. "Increased Automobile Fuel Efficiency and Synthetic Fuels: Alternative for Reducing Oil Imports." Office of Technology Assessment, Washington, D.C. (1982).

2. J. D. Bernal, *Science and Industry in the Nineteenth Century* (Bloomington and London: Indiana University Press, 1953).

3. W. Richard, "A Practical Treatise on the Manufacture and Distribution of Coal Gas" (London: E & F Spon, 1877).

4. M. Nord, *Textbook of Engineering Materials* (New York: John Wiley, 1952).

5. M. Berthelot, "Methode Universelle Pour Reduire et Saturer d'Hydrogene Les Composes Organiques," *Bulletin de la Société Chimique* 11 (1869): pp. 278–286.

6. A significant variety of sophisticated catalysts were used in the German DCL plants, as reviewed by the British Ministry of Fuel and Power, *Report on the Petroleum and Synthetic Oil Industry of Germany* (London: Ministry of Fuel and Power, His Majesty's Stationary Office, 1947).

7. Ibid.

8. M. Bar-Zahar, *The Hunt for German Scientists* (New York: Hawthorn Books, 1967).

9. M. C. Stopes, "Coal Liquefaction," *Philosophical Transactions of the Royal Society of London* B Series 90 (1919): 470–487.

10. P. Chiche, "Coal Properties, Resources and Utilization," in *Handbook of Coal Petrology,* 2nd Ed. (Paris: International Committee for Coal Petrology (ICCP), Centre National de la Recherche Scientifique, 1983).

11. S. Parkash, B. Ignasiak, and M. P. du Plessis, "Management of Coal Macerals with Liquefaction of Low Rank Coals," *Liquid Fuel Tech.* 1, no. 3 (1983): 219–233.

12. W. H. Wiser, "Research in Coal Technology: The University Role," in H. W. Sternbert (ed.) *Synfuels and Coal Energy Symposium* (Buffalo, NY: DOE Conf. 74190, 1986), pp. 57–72.

13. M. L. Gorbaty, "Challenges in Fossil Energy Chemistry," in L. Petrakis and J. P. Fraissard (eds.), *Magnetic Resonance: Introduction, Advanced Topics, and Applications to Fossil Energy* (Malene, Crete: NATO Advanced Study Institute on Magnetic Resonance, 1983; Dordrecht, The Netherlands: D. Reidel Publishing Co., 1984), pp. 203–218.

14. M. L. Gorbaty, F. J. Wright, R. K. Lyon, R. B. Long, R. H. Schlosberg, Z. Baset, R. Liotta, B. G. Silbernagel, and D. R. Neskora, "Coal Science, Basic Research Opportunities," *Science* 206, no. 4422 (1979): 1029–1034.

Chapter 5

1. G. K. Goldman, *Liquid Fuel From Coal* (Park Ridge, NJ: Noyes Data Corp., 1972), pp. 186–221.

2. P. Nowacki, *Coal Liquefaction Processes* (Park Ridge, NJ: Noyes Data Corp., 1979), pp. 15–17 and 22–75.

3. W. H. Wiser, "Conversion of Bituminous Coal to Liquids and Gases: Chemistry and Representative Processes," in L. Petrakis and J. P. Fraissard (eds.), *Magnetic Resonance: Introduction, Advanced Topics, and Applications to Fossil Energy* (Malene, Crete: NATO Advanced Study Institute on Magnetic Resonance, 1983; Dordrecht, The Netherlands: D. Reidel Publishing Co., 1984).

4. K. Grandy, *Coal Conversion Technologies,* (Springfield, IL: Illinois Dept. of Business and Economic Development, 1975).

5. L. J. Scotti, J. F. Jones, L. Ford, and B. D. McMunn, "The Project COED Pilot Plant," *Chem. Eng. Prog.* 71, no. 4 (1975): 119–120.

6. J. R. Longanbach and F. Bauer, "Fuels and Chemicals by Pyrolysis," ACS Meeting (Philadelphia, PA: Garnett Research and Development Company, April 1975).

7. A. Sass, "Garrett's Coal Pyrolysis Process," *Chem. Eng. Prog.* 70 (Jan. 1974).

8. K. A. Schowalter and N. S. Boodman, "The Clean Coke Process for Metallurgical Coke," *Chem. Eng. Prog.,* Technical Manual, Coal Processing Technology (1974).

9. F. B. Carlson, L. H. Yardumian, and M. T. Atwood, "The TOSCOAL Process For Low Temperature Coal Pyrolysis," *Chem. Eng. Progress,* Technical Manual, Coal Processing Technology (1974).

10. ERDA 79-96/4.

11. "Coal Conversion," 1977 Technical Report, USDOE, DOE/ET-0061/1 (June 1978).

12. M. Steinberg, T. V. Sheehan, and Q. Lee, "Flash Hydropyrolyses Process for Conversion of Lignite to Liquid and Gaseous Products," Brookhaven National Laboratory, BNL 20915 (October 1975).

13. Ibid.

14. I. Howard Smith and G. J. Werner, *Coal Conversion Technology* (Park Ridge, NJ: Noyes Data Corporation, 1976).

15. R. W. Ranmler, "The Retorting of Coal, Oil Shale, Tar Sand by Means of Circulated Fine-Grained Heat Carriers as a Preliminary State in the Production of Synthetic Crude Oil," AIME Annual Meeting, Denver (February 1970).

16. P. Nowacki, *Coal Liquefaction Processes* (Park Ridge, NJ: Noyes Data Corp., 1979).

17. I. Howard Smith and G. J. Werner, *Coal Conversion Technology,* op. cit.

18. W. H. Wiser, "Conversion of Bituminous Coal to Liquids and Gases," op. cit.

19. Solids tend to present as colloidal suspensions in the liquid product. Thus, their removal is difficult unless the solids can be agglomerated to form more filterable particle sizes.

20. L. E. Furlong, et al., "Coal Liquefaction by the Exxon Donor Solvent Process," AIChE National Meeting, Los Angeles, California (November 18, 1975).

21. "Coal Conversion," US DOE, DOE/ET-0061/1, Wash., D.C. (June 1978).

22. R. M. Eccles, G. R. De Vaux, and B. Dutkiewicz, "Current Status of H-Coal Commercialization," Synthetic Fuel Symposium, Chicago, Illinois (May 1–2, 1980).

23. H. H. Stoller, J. B. MacArthur, and G. G. Comolli, "Current Status of H-Coal Commercialization," Seventh Annual International Conference on Coal Gasification, Liquefaction, and Conversion to Electricity, Pittsburgh, Pennsylvania (August 5–7, 1980).

24. Personal communication, Marvin Greene (Lummus Crest, Inc., Bloomfield, N.J.) to W. Meyer (December 2, 1986).

25. These include Lummus' integrated two-stage liquefaction (Lummus ITSL), Wilsonville integrated two-stage liquefaction (Wilsonville, ITSL), Wilsonville reconfigured integrated two-stage liquefaction (Wilsonville RITSL), the modified Lummus integrated two-stage liquefaction (Modified Lummus ITSL), AMOCO integrated two-stage liquefaction (AMOCO), and HRI's catalytic two-stage liquefaction (CTSL).

Chapter 6

1. See L. R. Hellwig, et al., "The H-Oil Process: A New Refining Technique," American Petroleum Institute, *Proceedings* 42 (1962): 218–230.

2. See S. B. Alpert, et al., "Can Coal Compete for Liquid Fuels?" *Hydrocarbon Processing* 43 (November 1964): 193–197.

3. PL 86-599, 74 Stat. 336.

4. See Craufurd D. Goodwin (ed.), *Energy Policy in Perspective* (Washington, D.C.: The Brookings Institution, 1981), pp. 266–269.

5. U.S. Congress, House Appropriations Committee. Department of Interior and Related Agencies Appropriations for 1969. Part 2, March 5, 1968.

6. U.S. Congress, House Appropriations Committee. Department of Interior and Related Agencies Appropriations for 1968. Part 2, March 1, 1967.

7. See Coal Age's *New Handbook of Surface Mining* (New York: McGraw-Hill, 1981), p. 353.

8. See Francis W. Richardson, *Oil from Coal* (Park Ridge, NJ: Noyes Data Corporation, 1975).

9. E. T. Layng and K. C. Hellwig, "Liquid Fuels from Coal by the H-Coal Process," *Mining Congress Journal* 55 (April 1969): 64–65.

10. Ashland Synthetic Fuels Inc., personal communication (September 2, 1982).

11. John Mitchell, Kentucky Department of Energy, personal communication (September 1, 1982).

12. Harry S. Newman, "H-Coal Pilot Plant Phase II Construction and Phase III Operation Management Plan." Ashland Synthetic Fuels Inc. (October 20, 1977), p. 3.

13. Ashland Synthetic Fuels, Inc. "H-Coal Pilot Plant Phase II Construction and Phase III Operations: Environmental Plan." Prepared for the U.S. Department of Energy (August 15, 1978), p. 1.

14. See Walter Baer, et al., "Analysis of Federally Funded Demonstration Projects: Supporting Case Studies." Prepared for the Experimental Technology Program, U.S. Department of Commerce (Santa Monica, CA: Rand Corporation, April 1976), pp. K33–K44.

15. Robert Tippee, "Ashland: Push Commercialization of All Synfuel Technologies," *Oil and Gas Journal* 77 (August 20, 1979): 60.

16. A commercial plant is expected to employ seven reactors. These scale-up factors are based on the capacity for one of the reactors.

17. U.S. Congress, General Accounting Office, "Controlling Federal Costs for Coal Liquefaction Program Hinges on Management and Contracting Improvements" (Washington, D.C.: U.S. General Printing Office, February 4, 1981).

18. Ibid., p. 54.

19. U.S. Department of Energy, Office of the Inspector General. Report on the Inspection of the H-Coal Pilot Plant Project. Report Number INS 79-5, March 31, 1979.

20. Ibid., p. 2.

21. See Ashland Synthetic Fuels, Inc. "H-Coal Pilot Plant Phase II Construction and Phase III Operation: Monthly Report for August 1977" (September 17, 1977), p. 2.

22. General Accounting Office, "Controlling Federal Costs," p. 16.

23. Office of the Inspector General, "Report on the Inspection of the H-Coal Project," p. 5.

24. The term "hand off failure" was taken from Edward W. Merrow, et al., "A Review of Cost Estimation in New Technologies: Implications for Energy Process Plants" (Santa Monica, CA: Rand Corporation, July 1979), p. 81.

25. General Accounting Office, "Controlling Federal Costs," p. 15.

26. Merrow, et al., "A Review," op. cit., p. 82.

27. Hydrocarbon Research Inc., "Project H-Coal: Report on Process Development." Prepared for the Office of Coal Research (December 1968).

28. U.S. Department of the Interior, Bureau of Mines, "Preliminary Economic Assessment of H-Coal Process Producing 50,000 Barrels Per Day of Liquid Fuels from Two Coal Seams: Wyodack and Illinois," ERDA 76-56, Morgantown, West Virginia (March 1976).

29. Dick Olliver, *Oil and Gas from Coal* (London: Financial Times Business Information, 1981).

30. A plant is considered a pioneer if it introduces on a commercial scale a new product or process, or if a large scale-up from prior commercial size is involved. See Merrow, et al., "A Review," op. cit., pp. 95–110.

31. Energy Security Act, PL 96-294.

32. "Ashland Affirms Commitment to H-Coal Commercial and Pilot Plants," *Synfuels* (February 3, 1982): 6.

33. Each private sponsor needed to put up $100–150 million to ensure a sound financial package.

34. Mike Brown, "Ashland Oil Kills Plan for Synthetic Fuel Plant in Breckinridge County," *Louisville Courier-Journal* (November 23, 1982).

35. "AIRCO Unlikely to Pick Up H-Coal," *Platt's Oilgram News* 60 (November 30, 1982): 5.

36. Ashland Oil press release reported in *Platt's Oilgram News* 60 (November 23, 1982): 5.

37. The data in this section were gathered from a variety of sources including: Ashland Synthetic Fuels, Inc. and AIRCO Energy Company, Inc., The Breckinridge Project Initial Effort Report VIII (prepared for U.S. DOE under Cooperative Agreement No. DE-FC05-800R20717, 1981) and Abu Talib, David Gray, and Martin Neuworth, "Assessment of H-Coal Process Development," prepared by the Mitre Corporation for the U.S. Department of Energy, Contract No. DE-AC01-80ET13800, 1984.

38. Ashland Synthetic Fuels, Inc. and AIRCO Energy Company, Inc., "The Breckinridge Project Initial Effort Report VIII," Prepared for U.S. DOE under Cooperative Agreement No. DE-FC05-800R20717, 1981.

39. Edward W. Merrow, Kenneth E. Phillips, and Christopher W. Myers, *Understanding Cost Growth and Performance Shortfalls in Pioneer Process Plants* (Santa Monica, CA: The Rand Corp., 1981).

40. Talib, Gray, and Neuworth, "Assessment of H-Coal Process Development," op. cit.

41. Ashland Synthetic Fuels Inc., personal communication (September 2, 1982).

42. See Office of the Inspector General, "Report on the Inspection of the H-Coal Pilot Plant Project," and U.S. General Accounting Office, "Controlling Federal Costs."

43. *Oil Daily* (November 13, 1985), p. 4.

Chapter 7

1. Hearings of the U.S. House of Representatives Committee on Interior and Insular Affairs, Subcommittee on Mines and Mining, "Briefing Session with Director," Office of Coal Research (May 7, 1969).

2. Congressional Research Service, Costs of Synthetic Fuels in Relation to Oil Prices, Report to the U.S. House of Representatives, Committee on Science and Technology (Washington, D.C.: USGPO, 1981).

3. Congressional Research Service, Costs of Synthetic Fuels in Relation to Oil Prices, Report to the U.S. House of Representatives, Committee on Science and Technology (Washington, D.C.: USGPO, 1981).

4. Dick Kirschten, "Gasoline from Coal: South Africa Proves It Takes Time," *National Journal* (August 8, 1979): 1410–1412.

5. Statement of Paul Ignatius, Eugene Zuckert, and Lloyd Cutler before the U.S. Senate Government Affairs Committee, July 17, 1979.

6. Testimony of Harold Ickes before the U.S. Senate Subcommittee of the Committee on Public Lands and Surveys in connection with S. 1243, a bill authorizing the construction and operation of demonstration plants to produce synthetic fuels, August 3, 1943.

7. This is not to suggest that industrial decision makers are driven only by profit motives. A recent survey of energy company executives indicated that while national security is clearly a secondary (to profits and market conditions) factor in decisions to invest in synfuels project, it is one of the factors weighed in investment decisions. For additional information on investment motives and patterns, see Peter Huessy, "Historical, Current, and Projected Trends in Private Sector R&D Investment in Oil Shale and Coal Liquefaction Technologies," prepared for the National Science Foundation, Contract #43877, May 1982.

8. Comments during hearings of the U.S. House of Representatives Committee on Interior and Insular Affairs, May 7, 1969.

9. Testimony of W. Bowman Cutter before Senate Subcommittee on Energy and Power, Committee on Interstate and Foreign Commerce, October 18, 1979.

10. C. J. Wurdock, "Projecting Demographic Impacts of Synfuel/Power Plant Construction in Western Kentucky: 1982–1990" (Louisville, KY: University of Louisville, Urban Studies Center, February 1982).

11. Ibid.

12. S. Weiss and E. Gooding, "Estimation of Differential Employment Multipliers in a Small Region Economy," *Land Economics* 44 (1968): 235–244.

13. W. Brown and H. Kahn, "Prices of Synthetic Fuels: Can They Be Competitive?" Testimony prepared for the U.S. House of Representatives, Committee on Science and Technology, September 13, 1979, p. 7.

14. D. Goodman, Testimony before the U.S. House of Representatives, Interstate and Foreign Commerce Committee, Oct. 11, 1979.

15. *Platt's Oilgram News* (November 23, 1982), p. 6.

16. *Industry Surveys* (August 21, 1986), p. 7.

17. Peter Huessy, "Historical, Current, and Projected Trends," op. cit.

18. E. Merrow, K. Phillips, and C. Myers, *Understanding Cost Growth and Performance Shortfalls in Pioneer Process Plants* (Santa Monica, CA: The Rand Corp., 1981).

19. Ibid.

20. C. Myers and R. F. Shangraw, *Understanding Process Plant Schedule Slippage and Start-up Costs* (Santa Monica, CA: The Rand Corp., 1984).

21. R. S. Kaplan, *Tax Policies for R&D and Technological Innovation* (Washington, D.C.: NTIS, 1975), p. 17.

22. For an empirical analysis of potential "crowding out" of incentives, see R.

Angell and A. Link, "R&D Incentives and the Economic Recovery Tax Act of 1981," mimeo, 1983.

Chapter 8

1. See letter from W. S. Farish, then president of Standard Oil Co., dated 7/15/42 and directed to the Subcommittee on Mines and Mining of the House of Representatives.

2. R. Vietor, "The Synthetic Liquid Fuels Program," op. cit., 1980, 1984.

3. For details of an analysis of 1982 industry perception, see M. M. Crow, "Synthetic Fuels Development: The Impact of the Reagan Administration," Syracuse University Institute for Energy Research (Policy Series 82-3, December 1982).

4. Ibid.

5. Some observers do, however, concern themselves with the nature of the policy instrument. One of the interviewees for this project commented: "In general, the only meaningful help to get industry involved is to offer them tax incentives. . . . DOE has had some influence but in the future they will have trouble convincing industry that their investment will pay off. In general, tax incentives are more attractive to industry than direct support of particular work."

6. See, for example, Chubin and Studer, *The War on Cancer* (Beverly Hills, CA: Sage, 1983).

Chapter 9

1. R. Rothwell and W. Zegveld, *Industrial Innovation and Public Policy* (London: Frances Pinter, 1981).

2. J. E. Schnee, "Government Programs and the Growth of High-Technology Industries," *Research Policy* 5, no. 1 (1977): 2–24.

3. Some ways in which the U.S. and South African experience diverge: the South African air quality standards are more lax, the South Africans' indigenous petroleum reserves are modest, and South Africa has taken several steps to prop up the price for coal liquids.

4. Congressional Research Service, "Costs of Synthetic Fuels in Relation to Oil Prices" (Washington, D.C.: Congressional Research Service, March 1981).

5. National Petroleum Council, *Final Report* (Washington, D.C.: U.S. Department of Interior, 1953).

6. National Research Council, *Refining Synthetic Liquids from Coal and Shale: Final Report of the Panel on R&D Needs in Refining of Coal and Shale Liquids,* Energy Engineering Board, Assembly of Engineering (Washington, D.C.: National Academy Press, 1980).

7. D. D. Whitehurst, *Coal Liquefaction: The Chemistry and Technology and Thermal Processes* (New York: Academic Press, 1980).

8. Bernard S. Lee, *Synfuels From Coal* (New York: N.Y. Aiche Monograph Series No. 14, Vol. 78, 1982).

9. T. J. Polaert, "Status of German Coal Conversion Technology," *Chemical Economy and Engineering Review* 17, no. 3 (March, 1985): 12–22.

10. "The Dirty Face of Coal," *Science News* (September 17, 1983).

11. P. F. Rothberg, "SFC and National Synthetic Fuels Policy," *Congressional Research Service Review* (September 1984), pp. 23–36.

12. *Congressional Research Service* (1981), op. cit.

13. R. Nelson and R. Langlois, "Innovation Policy: Lessons from American History," *Science* 219 (February 1983): 817–818.

14. U. Desai, and M. M. Crow, "Failures of Power and Intelligence in Government Decision Making," *Administration and Society* 5, no. 2 (August 1983): 185–206.

15. M. M. Crow, and G. L. Hager, "Political Versus Technical Risk Reduction and the Failure of U.S. Synthetic Fuel Development Efforts," *Policy Studies Review* 5, no. 1 (August 1985): 145–152.

16. R. Vietor, "The Synthetic Liquid Fuels Program: Energy Politics in the Truman Era," *Business History Review* 54, no. 1 (Spring 1980): 1–34. D. E. Kash and R. Rycroft, *U.S. Energy Policy: Crisis and Complacency* (Norman, OK: University of Oklahoma Press, 1984).

17. R. R. Nelson and R. N. Langlois, "Innovation Policy: Lessons from American History," *Science* (February 18, 1983): 817–818.

18. J. R. Rudolph and S. Willis, "The Politics of Technology, Public Policy, and Administration: The Synthetic Fuels Venture in Western Democracies," presented at the American Political Science Association annual meeting in New Orleans, Louisiana (August 1985).

19. U. Desai and M. M. Crow, "Failures of Power and Intelligence in Government Decision-making," op. cit.; G. S. C. Wang, "Evolution of a Synfuels Project: An Engineer's Perspective," Proceedings of the IASTED Energy Symposia, Anaheim, California (1981); International Energy Agency, *Coal Liquefaction: A Technology Review* (Paris: Organization for Economic Cooperation and Development, 1982); S. S. Penner, *Assessment of the Long-Term Research Needs for Coal Liquefaction Technologies* (FERWG-11) (Washington, D.C.: U.S. Department of Energy).

20. D. Olliver, *Oil and Gas from Coal* (London: Financial Times Business Information Ltd., 1981), p. 127.

21. The U.S. Synthetic Fuels Corporation was abolished April 18, 1986, pursuant to the Consolidated Omnibus Budget Reconciliation Act of 1985 (Public Law 99-272). That law transferred the responsibility of monitoring current synthetic fuels projects to the Office of the Secretary of the Treasury. In addition, on April 19, 1986, the Secretary of the Treasury established the Office of Synthetic Fuels Projects to monitor, technically and environmentally, current federally funded synthetic fuels projects.

22. Research and development funding for synthetic fuels research dropped, in constant 1974 dollars, from a high in 1981 of $377.6 million to a low level of less than $20 million total in FY 1987. The funding level is the lowest annual federal commitment to research and development activities related to liquefaction and gasification of coal since the 1960s. Essentially, the funding level for the research and development activities sponsored by the federal government has been returned to the pre-energy crisis level.

23. For a summary of the four major thrusts, see M. M. Crow and G. L. Hager, "Political vs. Technical Risk Reduction and the Failure of U.S. Synthetic Fuel Development Efforts," *Policy Studies Review* 5, no. 1 (August 1985): 145–152.

24. For an excellent summary of the politics surrounding energy technology

in general and synthetic fuels specifically, see W. A. Rosenbaum, *Energy, Politics, and Public Policy* (Washington, DC: Congressional Quarterly Inc., 1981).

25. For a good summary of the ebb and flow of public policy surrounding synthetic fuels technology development, see Joseph R. Rudolph and Sebrina Willis, "The Politics of Technology, Public Policy and Administration: The Synthetic Fuels Adventure in Western Democracies," paper presented at the 1985 Annual Meeting of American Political Science Association.

26. R. W. Hess, "Potential Production Cost Benefit of Constructing and Operating First of a Kind Synthetic Fuel Plants," Report N-2274-SFC (Santa Monica, CA: The Rand Corp., March 1985a); C. W. Myers and R. Y. Arguden, "Capturing Pioneer Plant Experience: Implications for Synfuel Projects," Report N-2063-SFT (Santa Monica, CA: The Rand Corp., Jan. 1984); R. W. Hess, "Review of Cost Improvement Literature with Emphasis on Synthetic Fuel Facilities and the Petroleum and Chemical Process Industries," Report N-2273-SFC (Santa Monica, CA: The Rand Corp., March 1985b); E. W. Merrow, K. E. Phillips, and C. W. Myers, "Understanding Growth and Performance Problems in Pioneer Process Plants," Report R-2569-DOE (Santa Monica, CA: The Rand Corp., June 1981).

27. R. W. Hess, "Review of Cost Improvement Literature," op. cit.

28. R. W. Hess, Potential Production Cost Benefit," op. cit., p. 2.

29. M. B. Lieberman, "The Learning Curve: Pricing and Market Structure in the Chemical Processing Industries." Ph.D. Thesis, Harvard University, Cambridge, Mass., 1982.

30. C. W. Myers and R. Y. Arguden, "Capturing Pioneer Plant Experience: Implications for Synfuel Projects," Report N-2063-SFT (Santa Monica, CA: The Rand Corp., Jan. 1984).

31. M. Crow and B. Bozeman, "A New Typology for R&D Laboratory Variation in the 1980s: Some Implications for Policy Analysts," *Journal of Policy Analysis and Management* 6, no. 3 (Spring 1987): 328–341; A. N. Link, "The Impact of Federal R&D Spending on Productivity," *IEEE Transactions on Engineering Management* EM-29 (1979): 166–169.

32. T. P. Hughes, "Technological Momentum in History: Hydrogenation in Germany 1898–1933. *Past and Present* 44 (August 1969): 106–133.

33. E. E. Donath, "Hydrogenation of Coal and Tar," in H. H. Lowry (ed.), *Chemistry of Coal Utilization* (supplemental volume) (New York: John Wiley, 1963).

34. T. P. Hughes, "Technological Momentum," op. cit., pp. 106–133.

35. Ibid., p. 130.

36. E. E. Donath, "Hydrogenation of Coal and Tar," op. cit.

37. U. Desai and M. M. Crow, "Failures of Power and Intelligence," op. cit.

38. G. M. Steinberg, "Comparing Technological Risks in Large Scale National Projects," *Policy Sciences* (1985): 80–93.

39. W. H. Lambright, M. M. Crow, and R. Shangraw, "National Projects in Civilian Technology," *Policy Studies Review* 3, nos. 3–4 (May 1984): 453–459.

INDEX

American Oil Company, 78,
American Petroleum Institute (API),
126
Arch Minerals Corporation, 68–69
Ashland Oil, 68–69; economic pressures on, 80–81
Aspinall, Wayne, 87
Atlantic Richfield Corporation
(ARC), 68–69, 100

baseline case example: of H-coal, 32–35, 63–85. *See also* H-coal
Bechtel Corporation, 77–81
Berthelot, M., 39, 41
boundary-setting: technology assessment and, 19–21
Breckinridge project. *See* H-coal,
baseline case example
Brookhaven National Laboratory
flash hydropyrolysis ignite process,
54

carbonization. *See* pyrolysis
Catalytic hydrogenation, 56–57
CFS two-stage liquefaction, 8
char-to-energy development (COED),
52–53
Chevron Oil, 100
Cities Services and Development Corporation, 65
coal: chemical byproducts, 40–41;
chemical byproducts, early manufacturing plant construction and,
41–43; chemical composition of,
45–46; chemists who contributed
to study of, 41; hydrogenation of,
42–43; mineralogy of, 44–45; solvent extraction and, 46, 54–56. *See
also* direct coal liquefaction (DCL)
Coalcon process, 53
coke, early uses of, 38–39
Consolidated Oil Company, 68
Cutler, Lloyd, 91

Department of Energy (DOE), 77–79
direct coal liquefaction: alternatives
to, 8–9; catalytic hydrogenation,
56–57; clean fuel and competitiveness, 91–92; COED process,
52–53; competitiveness of with
conventional fuels, 88–93; development of, 1–12; development of,
and hiatus effect, 143–46; early
manufacturing plant construction,
41–43; economics of, 87–111; economics of, and cost growth, 102–3;
economics of, and direct incentive
programs, 109–10; economics of,
and government subsidies, 107–10;
economics of, and industry economics, 100–4, 134; economics of,
and macroeconomics, 94–100; economics of, and models, 27–29; economics of, and patents as
indicators, 105–7; economics of,
and plant performance, 104; economics of, and regional economic
impact and, 92–93; economics of,
and return on investment, 104; economics of, and tax incentives,
107–9; effects of support hiatus
on, 131–46; failure to compete,
88–93, 135–38; firm-level economics of investment, 102–5; hiatus effects, 131–46; history of, after
1944, 49–61, 114–24; history of,
pre-1939, 37–47; industry economics and investment in, 100–5, 134;
inflation and costs of, 94–96; input/output analyses, 87–90; limited
success of, 43–46; macroeconomics
of, 94–100; models for explaining
DCL, 27–32; national security and,
91–92; Office of Coal Research
(OCR), 6–9, 65, 70, 87, 117–20;
oil crisis and, 3, 9–11, 120–22; oil
prices and competitiveness of, 87–

About the Authors

MICHAEL CROW is Director of Science Policy and Research, Iowa State University. He received his Ph.D. from Syracuse University.

BARRY BOZEMAN is Director of the Technology and Information Policy Program, Syracuse University. He received his Ph.D. from Ohio State University.

WALTER MEYER is Director of the Institute for Energy Research, Syracuse University. He received his Ph.D. from Oregon State University.

RALPH SHANGRAW, JR. is Senior Research Fellow, Technology and Information Policy Program, Syracuse University. He received his Ph.D. from Syracuse University.